BEFORE I DO:

Complete Premarital Counseling Workbook for Heterosexual, LGBTQ, and Polyamorous Partner(s)

OLIVIA L BAYLOR, LCPC, NCC, DCC

Copyright © 2017 Olivia L Baylor

All rights reserved. This book or parts thereof may not be reproduced in any form, stored in any retrieval system, or transmitted in any form by any means—electronic, mechanical, photocopy, recording, or otherwise—without prior written permission of the publisher, except as provided by United States of America copyright law.

ISBN-13: 978-1976245350

ISBN-10: 1976245354

Library of Congress Control Number: 2017916417

This is a work of fiction. Names, characters, places, and incidents either are the products of the author's imagination or are used fictitiously. Any resemblance to actual persons, living or dead, businesses, companies, events or locales is entirely coincidental.

Credits, references and permissions are listed on the same page of the items posted and are considered a continuation of the copyright page.

First Printing November 2017

CreateSpace Independent Publishing Platform, North Charleston, SC

For permission requests, write to Olivia L Baylor, at BaylorBook@gmail.com.

THIS PAGE INTENTIONALLY LEFT BLANK

TABLE OF CONTENTS

INTRODUCTION & THANK YOU 6

MY GOAL & PLEASE NOTE 7

MARRIAGE PREPARATION… 8

INFIDELITY 28

HOUSEHOLD ROLES… 37

CHORES… 42

FRIENDSHIP… 49

SEX/INTIMACY 54

FINANCES… 59

CHILDREN… 66

DEATH AND DYING… 80

SECOND MARRIAGES… 93

POLYAMORY PARTNER(S) 100

DISABILITY/ILLNESS… 112

PERSONAL SPACE/QUALITY TME 120

INTERRACIAL RELATIONSHIPS… 126

INTERRELIGIOUS RELATIONSHIPS 130

STEP-CHILDREN 135

©Olivia L Baylor LCPC, NCC, DCC

INFERTILITY/PMAD 141

IN-LAWS… 151

COMMUNICATION… 157

MILITARY PARTNER(S). 166

SUICIDE 169

SELF-ESTEEM 180

DOMESTIC VIOLENCE 186

ADDICTION… 193

YOU DID IT 199

INTRODUCTION

When I first started this workbook, I looked around for books that challenged couples and told the story of how marriages work. In my search, I noticed the materials were dated and didn't include information on LGBTQ relationships. The following questions came to mind. Why were all of the pronouns "she" and "he" and not "she" and "she"? Why are pronouns even used? Or why don't they discuss rules in polyamorous relationships? I decided to address these issues and take action by creating a workbook that is user friendly, gender neutral, and client focused. I'm hoping that you enjoy this book and find it helpful in the venture of your own relationship or to use with your clients.

THANK YOU

I have to thank some people for helping me with the journey of this workbook. I especially have to thank my family for giving me the space and time to complete this workbook. A special thank you to my mother Evelyn Linton for allowing me to use her poetry. Lauren Aycock Anderson for creating this beautiful cover, thank you. I also have to thank my family, therapists, partner(s) and friends who reviewed my workbook and gave me valuable information to make the necessary changes within it.

MY GOAL

My goal for this workbook is that it allows you to better understand your partner and your relationship. My hope is that anyone can use this book no matter their gender, sexual orientation, educational level etc., within the privacy of their own home or with their therapist. I hope you use this book to evaluate your relationship and have a clearer understanding of it. In marriage/unity some of the smallest things can become an issue in your relationship(s). The ultimate goal with this book is that you realize that your marriage/unity isn't about your wedding day, it's about what comes after it.

PLEASE NOTE

I am a therapist however, please read this statement below:

This book and the content provided herein are simply for educational purposes and do not take the place of mental health advice from your therapist. Every effort has been made to ensure that the content provided in this book is accurate and helpful for our readers at publishing time. However, this is not an exhaustive treatment of the subjects. No liability is assumed for losses or damages due to the information provided. You are responsible for your own choices, actions and results. You should consult with your therapist for your specific questions and needs. There may be the possibility that this workbook triggers you as a person and client. Please note that you are completing this workbook at your own risk!

CHAPTER 1
MARRIAGE PREPARATION

MARRIAGE PREPARATION

"So many partner(s) prepare for the wedding day and never prepare for their actual marriage/unity. Do you know who you're marrying?"

Olivia L Baylor, LCPC, NCC, DCC

Marriage is the beginning of a journey to a lasting relationship together. When you receive the engagement ring you become excited and thrilled of the future and what will come next.... the wedding. For most partner(s) that includes finding the right outfit, DJ, hall, catering, and cake. It's essential to have all of these things to make your wedding the "perfect day," but you sometimes forget to make sure you're marrying the right person. Besides buying this workbook, how much have you spent on your marriage? Did you go to any type of premarital counseling? Have you communicated about life, death, and/or children? Did you discuss sex, intimacy, and in-laws? Have you seen your partner(s)'s credit report? My assumption to most of these questions is **"NO"**! As you begin to take the steps to work on your relationship, review the questions below to see just how well you know your partner.

DEFINITIONS

Marriage: According to Napier, [1] "Marriage involves learning to be both separate and together, learning to allocate power, learning to play and work together, and (for some) perhaps the greatest challenge of all. Learning to rear another generation."

Intimacy: According to Harway, [2] "A condition of mutual emotional and often intense closeness among peers."

---

[1] *Napier, A. Y. (2000), 145. Making a marriage. In W. C. Nichols, M. A. Pace-Nichols, D. S. Becvar, & A. Y. Napier (Eds.), Handbook of family development and intervention (pp. 145–170). New York: Wiley

[2] **Harway, M. (2005), 29. *Handbook of couples therapy.* Hoboken (NY): J. Wiley & Sons.

MARRIAGE PREPARATION WORKSHEET

Directions: Read the questions closely. Complete this worksheet separately, then take time this evening or this week to discuss your answers.

Infidelity:

Do you trust your partner(s)? _____

Do you have a clear understanding of what your partner(s) believes is cheating? _____

Have you ever cheated on your partner(s)? _____

Can you forgive your partner(s) for cheating? _____

Elaborate on your thoughts below:

_____

_____

_____

Household Roles: *(This section is different than the others as it will ask you to include the name of your partner(s). You will then answer the questions).*

Do you expect to follow the heteronormative definition of a "traditional" household role in your marriage? Why or why not?

_____

Who do you expect to do the cleaning? _____

Who do you expect to do the cooking? _____

Who do you expect to be the disciplinary one in the home? _____

Elaborate on your thoughts below:

_____
_____
_____

Chores:

Do you have plans for chores in your household? _____

Are you opposed to starting a chore chart for your partner(s)? _____

Do you know the cleaning expectations that your partner(s)? _____

Who is better at completing the chores at home? _____

Elaborate more on your thoughts below:

_____
_____
_____

Friendship:

Is it okay if your partner(s) has friends of the same or opposite sex? _____

Do you want to know all of your partner(s) friends? _____

Does your partner(s) have friends that you don't like? _____

Do you believe that your friends can influence your relationship in a positive/negative way? _____

If so, how? _____

©Olivia L Baylor LCPC, NCC, DCC

Elaborate on your thoughts below:

_____

_____

_____

Sex/Intimacy:

Are you a virgin? _____

How many sexual partner(s) do you have or had? _____

Do you have an allergy to latex? _____

Do you believe in using protection (condoms, birth control etc.)?

_____

Have you ever had unprotected sex?

_____

When was the last time you had unprotected sex?

_____

How long before or when do you feel it is okay to have unprotected sex with your partner(s)?

_____

Do you have an STD? _____

When was the last time you had a STD/HIV Test? _____

What were the results? _____

Would you be willing to get another STD/HIV test? _____

Is sex important to you? _____

Is intimacy important to you? _____

©Olivia L Baylor LCPC, NCC, DCC

Who do you expect to initiate sex? _____

How many days a week do you expect sex? _____

If you identify as asexual, does your partner(s) fully understand you? _____

Have you completely communicated about oral sex with your partner(s)?
_____

Have you completely communicated about anal sex with your partner(s)?
_____

Is it important to know your partner(s) sexual fantasy? _____

Have you explored your sexual fantasies together? _____

Do you appreciate or like phone sex? _____

Do you have a safe word? _____

Has your partner(s) respected your safe word? _____

Have you fully discussed your sexual needs with your partner(s)?
_____

Have all of your sexual needs been met? _____

Elaborate on your thoughts below:
_____
_____
_____

Finances:

Do you want to see your partner(s) credit report? _____

Do you want to share finances? _____

Do you want to share bank accounts? _____

Would you be okay with your partner(s) having a personal saving account?
_____

Do you have debt? _____

How much debt do you have? _____

Who do you expect to handle the finances in your home? _____ Would you be willing to co-sign/consolidate debt together? _____ Do you currently have a savings account? _____ Are you willing to sign a prenuptial agreement? _____ Elaborate on your thoughts below:

_____
_____
_____

Children:

How many children do you want to have? _____

If you are unable to physically birth your child(ren), is adoption an option? ___

Would you allow your partner(s) to carry your child? _____

If adoption is an option, does race matter? _____

If adoption is an option, do you prefer a newborn or an older child?
_____

If adoption is an option, would you adopt a physically disabled child?
_____

Is surrogacy an option for you or your partner(s)?
_____

If your child identifies within the LGBTQ+ community, would you be accepting of them? _____

If your child does not identify within the LGBTQ+ community, would you be accepting of them? _____

Who do you expect to care for the children? _____

Elaborate on your thoughts below:

_____

_____

_____

In-Laws:

Are there any underlying issues that you have or foresee with your in-laws?
_____

Do you see your in-law's relationship as healthy? _____

Do you have a good relationship with your in-laws? _____

Do you want a better relationship with your in-laws? _____

Do you expect your in-laws to discipline your child(ren)? _____

Do you feel as though your in-laws are too involved in your relationship?
_____

How much time is "too much" time for your in-laws to visit? _____

Do you want to have your in-laws move in with you? _____

If your in-laws experience bad health or need care, are you okay with providing assistance to them and allowing them to move in with you?
_____

Do you have any cultural beliefs in regards to your parents (i.e. moving in with you when you have children etc.)? _____

Would you be okay with your partner(s) interacting with their in-laws from previous marriages? _____

Elaborate on your thoughts below:

_____
_____
_____

Death and Dying:
Are you afraid of death? _____
Do you have a plan for your passing? _____
Are you for/against having a Do Not Resuscitate (DNR)? _____
Do you have religious requirements that must be respected during your death? _____
Elaborate on your thoughts below:

_____
_____
_____

Second Marriages:
_____
Have you been married before? _____
Do you respect, believe or acknowledge the notion of marriage? _____
Do you have closure from your previous marriage? _____
Why you believe this relationship will be different? Elaborate on your thoughts. _____

©Olivia L Baylor LCPC, NCC, DCC

Elaborate on your thoughts below:

_____
_____
_____

Polyamory Partner(s):

Do you confirm to the belief of having a primary partner(s)? If so who is that person(s)? _____

(Non-Polyamory Couples) Have you ever considered having a polyamorous relationship? _____

Why did begin a polyamory relationship? _____
_____

Do you love/like all of your partner(s)? _____

After marriage do you expect more partner(s)? _____

Elaborate on your thoughts below:

_____
_____
_____

Disability/Illness:

Do you have any genetic illnesses in your family? _____

Have you ever cared for a family member with a disability? _____

Would you stay with your partner(s) if they became a person with a disability?
_____

Would you allow your in-laws to stay with you if they became a person with a disability?
_____

Elaborate on your thoughts below:

_____

_____

_____

Personal Space/Quality Time:

Do you still have "you time"? _____

Who gets more "individual time"? _____

Do you resent this? _____ If so, why? _____

What is something you like to do individually? _____

Elaborate on your thoughts below:

_____

_____

_____

Interracial Relationships:

Prior to this relationship have you been in an interracial relationship(s)?

_____

Have you reviewed your own internal bias/racism towards your partner(s) race/culture? _____ If so, what is it? _____

Has your relationship struggled with racism? _____

Are you worried about your children being discriminated against? _____

Elaborate on your thoughts below:

_____
_____
_____

Interreligious Relationships:

Prior to this relationship have you been in interreligious relationships?
_____

Have you reviewed your own internal bias/discriminatory views towards your partner(s) religion?_____ If so, what it is? _____

Has your relationship struggled with hatred towards you for dating outside of your religion(s)? _____

Are you worried about your children being discriminated against for their religious beliefs? Why or why not?
_____

What religion do you expect your children to practice? _____
Elaborate on your thoughts below:

_____
_____
_____

Infertility/PMAD:

Does infertility run in your family? _____

Does Postpartum Mood and Anxiety Disorder (PMAD) run in your family?
_____

©Olivia L Baylor LCPC, NCC, DCC

Currently, do you feel like you have support from your partner(s)? _____

Are you aware that PMAD can apply to both/all partner(s)? _____

Elaborate on your thoughts below:

_____

_____

_____

Communication:

Does your partner(s) communicate with you? If so how do they communicate (verbally, written etc.)? _____

On a scale of (1-10) with 1 being extremely effective and 10 being horrible, how would you rate communication in your relationship? _____

In conversations does your partner(s) talk over you? _____

Do you feel ignored after a conversation with your partner(s)? _____

Elaborate on your thoughts below:

_____

_____

_____

Step-Children:

Do you have a relationship with your step-child(ren) and their other parental figures? _____

Do you like your step-children? _____

Have you discussed your parental role in your step-child(ren)'s life with your partner(s)?_____

If so, what is it? _____

Would you be okay with your partner(s) being in contact with child(ren) from their previous relationship(s)?

_____

Elaborate on your thoughts below:

_____
_____
_____

Military Partners:

Has the military affected your relationship(s)? _____

If so, how? _____

How many deployments have you had? _____

Do you expect to deploy or go into training in the future? _____

How do you plan to keep intimacy during your deployment? _____

Who do you expect to initiate/maintain romance during your distance?

_____

Elaborate on your thoughts below:

_____
_____
_____

©Olivia L Baylor LCPC, NCC, DCC

MARRIAGE GOALS WORKSHEET

Directions: Read the questions closely. Complete this worksheet separately, then take time this evening or this week to discuss your answers.

Why do you want to marry your partner(s)?

_____

_____

_____

What are two goals that you have for your marriage within one year of being together?

1.

2.

What are two goals that you have for your marriage(s) within 5 years?

1.

2.

Write down 2 goals that you have for your marriage with buying this book.

1.

2.

MARRIAGE VALUES WORKSHEET

Directions: Read the questions closely. Complete this worksheet separately, then take time this evening or this week to discuss your answers.

What are the individual values that you have for yourself?

1.

2.

3.

4.

5.

What are the values that you have for your relationship?

1.

2.

3.

4.

©Olivia L Baylor LCPC, NCC, DCC

5.

What were the values that were instilled in you as a child?

1.

2.

3.

4.

5.

What are the values that you want to give to your child(ren)?

1.

2.

3.

4.

5.

MARRIAGE ASSUME WORKSHEET

Directions: Read the statement below. Complete this worksheet separately, then take time this evening or this week to discuss your answers.

Dear (Insert your name here),

As I begin to take steps in OUR relationship, I will be mindful not to ASSUME my partner(s) will know, understand or agree with everything that I want. I will acknowledge that we come from different households, with different morals, different beliefs, and different upbringings. When I ASSUME, I diminish the thought that my partner(s) is/are their own individual and therefore cannot read my mind. I will use this workbook without assuming for them, but rather learning with them.

Signed

_____

CHAPTER 2
INFIDELITY

INFIDELITY

"It's not the fact that you cheated, it's the meaning behind the cheating that is the real issue."

Olivia L Baylor, LCPC, NCC, DCC

Infidelity has been the cause of many relationships ending. One of the reasons why infidelity occurs is because many partners don't know how the other partner(s) identifies cheating. The number one response usually given in session about infidelity is, "I never knew that this was cheating". As the new era of internet usage and video chats have evolved so has the beliefs in cheating. As stated by Whisman & Wagers. [3]:

> "Relationships betrayals by which we refer to violations of expectations for emotional and physical exclusivity with one's partner. People involved in a romantic relationship most often expect to have certain needs met exclusively by their romantic partner. Infidelity, affairs and other forms of sexual and emotional betrayal violates such expectations of exclusivity."

---

[3] Whisman, M.A. & Wagers, T. P. (2005 p. 1384). Assessing relationship betrayals. Journal of Clinical Psychology: In Session, 61, 1383-1391. doi: 10.1002/jclp.20188

Consider if your partner wanted to cheat? Is it because they're missing something in the relationship? Does your partner(s) have a history of cheating? Did your partner(s) ever tell you why? If cheating has occurred or occurs in the future, can you forgive your partner(s)? Are you open to offering forgiveness? Forgiveness doesn't just mean a process of removing the pain, it also means a process of evaluating your relationship. The memory will always be present. In my practice, I created the acronym FORGIVE. Review the attached information to further understand how this can apply to your relationship.

HOW TO FORGIVE?

F = Fight through self-blame.

Limit the blame that you give to yourself and what you could have done to avoid the infidelity.

O = Openly communicate with your partner(s) regarding the relationship issues.

Communication is vital to having your partner(s) understand your needs. What was happening for the infidelity to occur?

R = Respond to their questions and acknowledge their feelings.

Acknowledge your partner(s) feelings regarding the infidelity. Console them when they need acknowledgement.

G = Give understanding and compassion.

Listen to the partner(s) who committed infidelity. Understand and listen to their reasoning.

I = Inspect your own self fault in the relationship.

Inspect the missing parts within the relationship that you contributed to.

V = Verify your thoughts on your relationship expectations.

Confirm and communicate with your partner(s) regarding what you expected in your relationship. See if they understand your values and expectations.

E = Evaluate your place in the relationship and your willingness to forgive.

Understand the expectations of your relationship and if forgiveness is an option.

©Olivia L Baylor LCPC, NCC, DCC

INFIDELITY WORKSHEET

Directions: Read the questions closely. Complete this worksheet separately, then take time this evening or this week to discuss your answers.

Do you think that it's cheating if you're physically intimate (vaginal penetration and/or anal penetration) with another individual and your partner(s) is not aware of the intimate interactions? _____

Do you think that it's cheating if you're orally (cunnilingus/fellatio) intimate with another individual and your partner(s) is not aware of the interactions?
_____

Do you believe that *emotionally* cheating is worse than *physically* cheating? Why or why not?
_____

Do you believe that having oral sex is worse than *emotionally* cheating? Why or why not?
_____

Do you believe that oral sex is worse than engaging in active penetration? Why or why not?
_____

Do you think it's cheating if your partner(s) looks at porn? Why or why not?
_____

Do you consider sexually explicit or emotionally explicit text messages with another person who is not your partner(s) to be cheating? Why or why not?

_____

(Polyamory Relationship) Do you consider going outside of your designated agreed upon terms or contract to be cheating? Why or why not?
_____

(Polyamory Relationship) If your partner(s) begins to date a non-polyamory person is that cheating? Why or why not?
_____

Do you consider flirting to be cheating? Why or why not?
_____

Is communicating verbally with someone in a sexual manner (phone sex) cheating? Why or why not?_____

Do you consider usage of sex toys in the absence of your partner(s) cheating? Why or why not? _____

©Olivia L Baylor LCPC, NCC, DCC

Do you consider fantasizing of other individuals during sexually intimate interactions to be cheating? Why or why not? _____

Elaborate on your thoughts below:

_____

_____

_____

APOLOGY LETTER TEMPLATE

Directions: Complete the following information to develop an apology letter to your partner(s). Once you have completed this letter, give it to them and communicate about your feelings regarding the infidelity.

Dear_____,

I apologize for_____. I want to express my sincere apology for not taking into consideration our relationship, your feelings, and your heart. I take full responsibility for my wrongdoings. I want to take the time to fully confess my wrongdoings to bring complete closure to the situation. I promise to build and gain your (our) trust again by doing the following things:

1.

2.

3.

4.

5.

I do these things not because you've asked me to do them. I do them because this relationship is too important for me to lose. I hope that this letter allows for you to see that I am truly sorry.

Sincerely,

_____

ACCEPTANCE LETTER TEMPLATE

Directions: Complete the following information to develop an acceptance letter to your partner(s). Once you have completed this letter give it to them and communicate about your feelings regarding the infidelity.

Dear_____,

I (WE) accept your apology for_____. I want to express my sincere acceptance and forgiveness to you and acknowledge how this has affected our relationship. I take full responsibility for any wrongdoings. I want to forgive you and bring complete closure to the situation. I promise not to bring up this infidelity as a form of attack on you or our relationship. I promise to allow you to build and gain your (our) trust again by doing the following things:

1.

2.

3.

4.

5.

I do these things not because you've asked me to do them. I do them because this relationship is too important for me to lose. I hope that this letter allows for you to see that I will begin the steps to forgive you.

Sincerely,

_____

CHAPTER 3
HOUSEHOLD ROLES

HOUSEHOLD ROLES

"Your expectations are not always your partner(s) reality."
Olivia L Baylor, LCC, NCC, DCC

Have you ever heard the saying, "you never know someone until you have lived with them?" Do you have certain beliefs and expectations for your household roles because of what you learned as a child? As you grow up you observe and internalize the roles within your household. What if you grew up in a polyamorous household? Did you view your parents as a shared partnership with one another? Did you see the poly family as a belief and a family that you wanted for yourself? Consider these roles and how they've affected you. Within those households you've experienced a way of life that you may find acceptable. In the heterosexual household, you may have experienced a mother or father. Their roles could've been what society considers to be "traditional roles", in which the mother would stay home and the father would work. The mother most likely filled the role of having emotional connection with their child(ren), while the father was more of the disciplinarian.[4] In either case you were exposed to some form of roles in your

---

[4] Ferris, K. (2016). *REAL WORLD: an introduction to sociology.* S.l.: W W NORTON.

household. You may feel as though those roles are essential to the life that you want. If you were raised in a LGBTQ+ household, roles are viewed differently. You may have had two parents who divided their roles evenly, or not considered household roles as a main factor in their lives. As a result, your household may have been an establishment in your choice on what you desire for your own household now. These are considerations and conversations to have with your partner(s) in order to have a clear understanding of your expectations.

HOUSEHOLD ROLES WORKSHEET

Directions: Read the questions closely. Complete this worksheet separately, then take time this evening or this week to discuss your answers.

What role did your first parental figure(s) take in your household? For example, did they cook, clean, etc.?

_____
_____

What role did your secondary parental figure take in your household? For example, did they mainly fix items, cut the grass, discipline the children, etc.?

_____
_____

What role did your other parental figure take in your household? For example, did they mainly do homework with you, play with you, etc.?

_____
_____

Do you have expectations for your partner(s) when it comes to your household?

_____
_____

What are your thoughts on sharing household responsibilities?

_____

_____

What type of roles did your parents have in their relationships that you liked and disliked?

_____

_____

Elaborate on your thoughts below:

_____

_____

CHAPTER 4
CHORES

CHORES

"You have cleaned the room, but arguments continue to arise about your cleaning habits. Is that because you did not clean the way that your partner(s) had expectations for?"

Olivia L Baylor, LCPC, NCC, DCC

Cleaning isn't fun, but someone has to do it. In my experience as a therapist working with partner(s), I've seen minimal issues such as cleaning up a cup, spiral into major issues. To reduce conflict, there's always the possibility of hiring someone to clean for you. However, this isn't always feasible for all families. So, what are some ways to fix the issues before it begins?

The first solution is to clean together. Cleaning together as a partner(s) brings a sense of completeness and understanding. When you clean together each of you learn what the other person expects for their household. This can drastically shift the relationship. Let's use the example of Alex and Cory.

Case Scenario:

It's chore day and Alex has to clean the bathroom. Cory typically cleans the bathroom, but Alex decides to take over today. When Alex goes into the bathroom they wipe down the counter, clean the inside of the toilet, and wash the inside of the bathtub. When Cory goes into the bathroom they observe this and says, "you didn't clean *anything!*"

There's definitely a false statement by Cory. Essentially, Alex did clean, but didn't clean to meet Cory's expectations.

How do you know exactly what your partner(s) wants? Cleaning together helps you understand your partner(s) expectations. Therefore, discussing chores may eliminate confusion or disappointment of expectations in the future.

EXTENSIVE CLEANING ROOM TO ROOM WORKSHEET

Directions: Review the checklist below. Check off the items that you believe should be completed every time that you clean. Once completed, take time this evening or this week to discuss your answers together.

LIVING ROOM	BATHROOM	KITCHEN
o Dust entire room o Vacuum (if you have carpet) o Mop floor o Wipe down walls o Vacuum chair(s) o Wash curtains o Wipe windows o Wipe down table(s)/ lamp(s) etc. o Clean ceiling fan o Wipe down doors o Wipe down baseboards o Organize DVD's o Wipe down TV	o Dust o Clean out bathroom closet o Put away towels o Wipe down sink o Clean inside of toilet o Clean top and bottom of toilet o Take expired meds out of cabinet and discard properly o Take out old toothpaste, mouthwash, floss and discard o Discard old makeup	o Clean out cabinets o Organize silverware drawer o Wash kitchen towels o Clean out oven o Clean backsplash o Take out trash o Clean inside of trash can o Clean inside of stove hood o Wipe down countertop o Wash dishes o Clean out dishwasher

o Change out filter o Dust photos	o Mop floor o Put new tissue on roller o Clean interior of shower o Check shower curtain for age and cleanliness o Replace air freshener o Clean air vent o Disinfect handles o Wipe down walls	o Put dishes in dishwasher o Mop floor o Change air freshener o Clean out filter o Wipe down walls o Disinfect handles o Clean ceiling fan o Clean out fridge o Wipe down fridge o Change water filter o Change arm and hammer o Wipe out microwave o Wipe out coffee pot
DINING ROOM	**BEDROOM**	**BASEMENT**
o Clean out cabinets o Wipe down cabinets o Wipe down walls o Wipe table down o Dust photos o Wipe or vacuum chairs o Mop floor	o Wash sheets o Change sheets o Wash curtains o Disinfect handles o Put away clothes o Wash clothes o Wipe down television	o Dust entire room o Vacuum (if you have carpet) o Mop floor o Wipe down walls o Vacuum chair(s) o Wash curtains o Wipe windows

©Olivia L Baylor LCPC, NCC, DCC

o Vacuum floors o Wash curtains o Wipe windows o Clean ceiling fan o Clean out vents	o Wipe down counter o Clean mirrors o Wipe down walls o Vacuum floor o Mop floor o Organize jewelry	o Wipe down table/ lamp etc. o Clean ceiling fan o Wipe down doors o Wipe down baseboards o Organize DVD's o Wipe down TV o Change out filter o Dust photos

CHORE CHART

Directions: Review the attached chore chart. Utilize it for one month to see if you're meeting each other's expectations with chores.

Rooms	Week 1	Initial	Week 2	Initial	Week 3	Initial	Week 4	Initial
Bathroom								
Living room								
Kitchen								
Bedroom								
Dining room								

CHAPTER 5
FRIENDSHIP

FRIENDSHIP

"Partner(s) can have combined friends, but you should also have individual friends. The problems in your relationship(s) begin to arise when you have toxic friends."

Olivia L Baylor, LCPC, NCC, DCC

In some aspect of your life you've experienced a connection with an individual that begins to blossom into some sort of a relationship. You essentially begin to call this person a friend. Having separate friends and separating yourself from your partner(s) friends at times is important to keep the interest between one another. Individuality gives each partner(s) autonomy so they don't feel they're completely defined by their relationship. However, being careful of your friend's role in your life is also very important.

Through my experience, I have seen that some friendships can cause conflicts within your own relationship. This can sometimes happen when friends know too much about your relationship and interfere by using their own personal life agenda. When your partner(s) does something that agitates or frustrates you, although sometimes tough, you forgive them. Friends are not as quick to do so. Do you expect or want your friend to know intimate information about your sex life? These are conversations that need to be discussed as a part of your marital rules. Complete the attached worksheet separately then work together to find out how involved you want your friends to be in your relationship.

FRIENDSHIP WORKSHEET

Directions: Read the questions closely. Complete this worksheet separately, then take time this evening or this week to discuss your answers.

How do you feel about your partner(s) having separate friends from you?

_____

_____

List 5 things that you believe are *off limits* for your partner(s) to discuss with friends?

1. _____
2. _____
3. _____
4. _____
5. _____

Do you currently have any issues with your partner(s) friends? _____

If so, who/whom? _____

Do you feel as though this relationship with your partner(s) friend can be salvaged? _____

©Olivia L Baylor LCPC, NCC, DCC

Why or why not? _____

Do you have any friends who you believe are toxic to your relationship?

_____

If so, who/whom? _____

Does your partner(s) have friends who you believe are toxic to your relationship? _____

If so, who/whom? _____

Do you feel as though your relationship could be affected by this friendship?

_____

If so, how? _____

Do you feel that it's important to have shared friends? _____

Elaborate on your thoughts below:

_____

_____

_____

CHAPTER 6
SEX/INTIMACY

SEX/INTIMACY

"Do you completely know what your partner(s) expects from sex?"

Olivia L Baylor, LCPC, NCC, DCC

Sex in a marriage is important. It allows for some people to express to their partner(s) that they love them. It also allows for the partner(s) to show that they're sexually attracted to them. Understanding how sex is connected to emotional attachment should be explored in order to see how it can affect your marriage/union. When it comes to sex/intimacy you have to consider your expectations. Have you ever talked about sex? For some people sex may not include penetration. For an individual who identifies within the LGBTQ+ community as asexual; for their partner(s), this can mean being intimate in other ways. For individuals who identify within the LGBTQ+ community as transgender, this may include communicating prior to sexual interaction to express comfort level with how sex is conducted. A number one question to ask your partner(s) is, what do they expect or want from sex? Do you really know how your partner(s) likes to have sex? Depending on your upbringing, past traumatic experiences, illnesses, and disabilities, sex doesn't look the same for each individual. However, it's similar in the way we communicate about it. Review the worksheet together and discuss your thoughts.

DEFINITIONS

Asexual

"Someone who does not experience sexual attraction."[5]

---
[5] General FAQ. (n.d.). Asexual Retrieved October 09, 2017, from http://www.asexuality.org/?q=general.html#ex1

SEX/INTIMACY WORKSHEET

Directions: Read the questions closely. Complete this worksheet separately, then take time this evening or this week to discuss your answers.

Have you discussed your sexual understanding with your partner(s)?
_____

On what days during the week do you expect to have sex? _____

How many times a day do you expect to have sex? _____

Do you expect oral sex during each sexual interaction? _____

Is role-play important to you? _____

Do you talk to your partner(s) about masturbation? _____

How do you feel about your partner(s) watching porn? _____

Do you feel sexually satisfied in your relationship? _____

Is there anything that you need sexually from your partner(s) that you aren't currently getting? _____

If so, what else do you need? _____

Is there anything sexually that you have wanted to do, but have not done with your partner(s)? _____

Have you engaged in phone sex with your partner(s)? _____

Have you tried role playing with your partner(s)? _____

Have you openly discussed a safe word with one another? _____

Do you feel comfortable sexually with your partner(s)? _____

Have you discussed anal sex and comfort with your partner(s)? _____

Do you want to use contraceptives during sex? _____

Are you okay with your partner(s) using sexual enhancement medication?
_____

Elaborate on your thoughts below:

_____
_____
_____

CHAPTER 7
FINANCES

FINANCES

"If YOU have no money then YOUR FAMILY has no money."

Olivia L Baylor, LCPC, NCC, DCC

Finances have been one of the highest reasons that some partner(s) have sought counseling in my practice. Some partner(s) struggle with having the discussion of how much debt is too much debt. Partner(s) sometimes avoid the discussion of what their credit score looks like. Finances typically come up once you consider buying a home, car, or investing in stocks. It's during this process, partner(s) realize their bills/debt are either too high, their credit is too low, or they have no credit at all. Every couple should always get a copy of their partner(s) credit report before walking down the aisle. Imagine walking down the aisle not knowing that your partner(s) has debt! What would you do after your married? Would you want to get a divorce? Would you consider fixing your credit together? Why not foreshadow that possibility now? Review the worksheets on the next page and remember that this is just a starting point to your credit endeavor. Consult with an attorney or a financial advisor to address your individual needs. These activities can help begin a discussion on how or what you want to do in order to fix your credit.

DEBT PAYOFF WORKSHEET

Directions: Include all items for the month that you pay. List the expense item, the amount due, the date due, and the amount remaining on your debt.

Debt	Amount Due	Due Date	Amount Remaining
		TOTAL DUE	
		TOTAL PAYCHECK	
		AMOUNT LEFT	

EXPENSE WORKSHEET

Directions: Include all items for the month that you pay. Complete this worksheet before and after pulling your credit report. List the total projected amount, the actual amount, the difference, and where it should be.

Item	Projected Cost	Actual Cost	Difference	Where it should be

CREDIT BUREAU INFORMATION

Directions: Review below the three credit bureau services. Contact them in reference to any information not properly listed on your credit report and to obtain a copy of your report.

Equifax

Equifax Credit Information Services, LLC

P.O. Box 740241, Atlanta, GA 30374

Experian

Experian National Consumer Assistance Center

P.O. Box 4500, Allen, TX 75013

TransUnion

TransUnion Consumer Relations

P.O. Box 2000, Chester, PA 19016-2000

GOALS WORKSHEET

Directions: Include all goals that you have for yourself as a couple. List the amount needed to obtain the goals. Complete the short-term and long-term goals that you feel that you will need. Communicate after completing this worksheet together.

SHORT TERM:

GOAL/ACTIVITY	DUE BY	CURRENT SAVINGS	NEED	DIFFERENCE	PUT ASIDE!
Buy Car	*September 2019*	*3,000.00*	*10,000.00*	*7,000.00*	*1,000.00 every Week/**month**/day*

LONG TERM:

GOAL/ACTIVITY	DUE BY	CURRENT SAVINGS	NEED	DIFFERENCE	PUT ASIDE!
Buy Car	*September 2019*	*3,000.00*	*10,000.00*	*7,000.00*	*1,000.00 every Week/**month**/day*

CHAPTER 8
CHILDREN

CHILDREN

"Do you have room in your heart, home, and life to give to another individual?"

Olivia L Baylor, LCPC, NCC, DCC

Children are a blessing when they come in one, two or multiple numbers. Having children for any couple/partner(s) would need to include some type of planning. Sometimes this planning includes surrogacy, adoption, natural childbirth, or kinship care. For some partner(s) it can be easy to have children, for others it may require a different route, such as surrogacy or adoption. Each of these scenarios include different financial and emotional strains. How much does it cost to raise a child? What about when it comes to disciplining your child(ren)? Do you understand your disciplining style? Let's try to touch a little bit on each question to prepare you for something that I call the "*unpreparable!*"

Financial Preparation for a child

Children are expensive! When preparing to support one you have to know where you financially stand. Realistically some individuals may not know this information when they get pregnant or give birth. Some people plan and some don't. Whichever the case, there's always the opportunity to prepare for the future of what could, should, may, or will be. This next set of worksheets will require you to do some outside homework on preparing, gathering information, and preparing numbers. This is not to scare you, but to prepare you. Consider this as a way to evaluate avenues of financial responsibility for when a child enters your family.

Disciplining Style

According to Rhee et al., [6] your disciplining style can affect the child in the long term. There are 4 different types of parenting styles. You have authoritarian, neglectful, authoritative, and permissive.[7] Your disciplining style can also be reviewed based on how you were raised at home by your parents. Complete this sections worksheet to understand your style and how sometimes your behavior could fall into the lines of abuse. There are different types of abuse. Verbal abuse, physical abuse, neglect, and emotional abuse.[8] Researching and having a clear understanding of how abuse can affect your child is vital to their development.

---

[6] Rhee, K.E., Lumeng J.C., Appugliese, D.P., Kaciroti, N., & Bradley, R.H. (2006). Parenting styles and overweight status in first grade. American Academy of Pediatrics (117), 6.

[7] Rhee, K.E., Lumeng J.C., Appugliese, D.P., Kaciroti, N., & Bradley, R.H. (2006). Parenting styles and overweight status in first grade. American Academy of Pediatrics (117), 6.

[8] Ferris, K. (2016). *REAL WORLD: an introduction to sociology.* S.l.: W W NORTON.

DEFINITIONS

Physical Abuse

"Is any intentional and unwanted contact with you or something close to your body."[9]

Emotional/Verbal Abuse

"Includes non-physical behaviors such as threats, insults, constant monitoring or "checking in," excessive texting, humiliation, intimidation, isolation or stalking."[10]

Authoritative

"Has clear expectations and consequences and is affectionate toward his or her child. The authoritative parent allows for flexibility and collaborative problem solving with the child when dealing with behavioral challenges. This is the most effective form of parenting."[11]

Authoritarian

"Has clear expectations and consequences, but shows little affection toward his or her child."[12]

Permissive

"Shows lots of affection toward his or her child but provides little discipline."[13]

---

[9] Is this abuse? www.loveisrespect.org/is-this-abuse/types-of-abuse/ on October 14, 2014
American Academy of Pediatrics: "Parenting Corner Q&A: Discipline," "Parenting Corner Q&A: Disobedience." American Academy of Child and Adolescent Psychiatry: "Discipline."

[10] Is this abuse? www.loveisrespect.org/is-this-abuse/types-of-abuse/ on October 14, 2014
American Academy of Pediatrics: "Parenting Corner Q&A: Discipline," "Parenting Corner Q&A: Disobedience." American Academy of Child and Adolescent Psychiatry: "Discipline."

[11] National Mental Health Association: "Strengthening Families Fact Sheet: Effective Discipline Techniques for Parents: Alternatives to Spanking."

[12] National Mental Health Association: "Strengthening Families Fact Sheet: Effective Discipline Techniques for Parents: Alternatives to Spanking."

[13] National Mental Health Association: "Strengthening Families Fact Sheet: Effective Discipline Techniques for Parents: Alternatives to Spanking."

CHILDREN FINANCIAL ACTIVITY

Directions: Review all of the possible items that come associated with a child(ren). Then review how financially stable as partner(s) preparing for child(ren) you need to be. **Do not view this as a sign to not have a child.** *Rather view this as a way to look at your finances and make some adjustments. First, list the items that you will need for your child. Then, complete the assumed cost of the items. Once those two sections are completed; go to your local large department store. Research and write up the actual cost of the items. Then return home and look at the difference. Use this as a level to understanding of your expectations versus your needs.*

Item Needed	Assumed Cost	Actual Cost	Difference

DISCIPLINING STYLE CHART

Directions: Review the disciplining style chart below. Talk to your partner(s) about where you fall within your disciplining style. Take this evening or this week to communicate your findings.

	High expectations for self-control	Low expectations for self-control
High sensitivity	**Authoritative:** Respectful of child's opinions, but maintains clear boundaries	**Permissive:** Indulgent, without discipline
Low sensitivity	**Authoritarian:** Strict disciplinarian	**Neglectful:** Emotionally uninvolved and does not set rules

[14]

---

[14] Rhee, K.E., Lumeng J.C., Appugliese, D.P., Kaciroti, N., & Bradley, R.H. (2006). Parenting styles and overweight status in first grade. American Academy of Pediatrics (117), 6.

DISCIPLINING STYLE WORKSHEET

Directions: Read the questions closely. Complete this worksheet separately, then take time this evening or this week to discuss your answers.

After reviewing your disciplining style, how do you feel about your upbringing?

_____

_____

_____

Which style do you most align with and why?

_____

_____

_____

Which style does your partner(s) most align with and why?

_____

_____

_____

©Olivia L Baylor LCPC, NCC, DCC

Elaborate on your thoughts below:

_____

_____

_____

CHILDREN WORKSHEET

Directions: Read the questions closely. Complete this worksheet separately, then take time this evening or this week to discuss your answers.

Do you think not having child(ren) would change your relationship?

_____

How many child(ren) do you want to have? _____

How would you feel if you're unable to have child(ren)? _____

_____

If you cannot have child(ren) is surrogacy an option? _____

How do you feel about adopting? _____

Do you believe that you could raise a child with a disability? _____

If not, please list the reasons why? _____

Is having children through IVF and option? Why or why not?

_____

Do you believe that your partner(s) should use any contraceptives during times that you do not want to have child(ren)?

_____

List your reasons for your answer. _____

What is something about the way that your parents disciplined you that you are okay with? _____

What is something that you would change? _____

Do you understand the different types of child abuse?
_____

Do you feel financially prepared for a child(ren)? _____

Elaborate on your thoughts below:

_____

_____

_____

SURROGATE NEEDS WORKSHEET

Directions: Read the questions closely. Complete this worksheet separately, then take time this evening or this week to discuss your answers.

Before looking into outside surrogacy, we would like to consider asking...?

_____ or _____ and _____

If _____ or _____ and _____

doesn't want to or cannot be our surrogate, here are some of the characteristics that we want in one:

Age?

_____

Race?

_____

Approximate distance to our home?

_____

Prefer if they have a child(ren) already?

_____

©Olivia L Baylor LCPC, NCC, DCC

Have to sign a contract?

_____

Evaluation from a psychiatrist?

_____

Criminal History?

_____

Physical fitness?

_____

Any nutritional requirements?

_____

Elaborate on your thoughts below:

_____

_____

_____

CHILDREN EXPECTATIONS WORKSHEET

Directions: Read the questions closely. Complete this worksheet separately, then take time this evening or this week to discuss your answers.

What are the expectations that you have for your child(ren)?

1.

2.

3.

4.

5.

If your child(ren) doesn't meet these expectations, is that okay? _____

If no, why not?

_____

_____

©Olivia L Baylor LCPC, NCC, DCC

Elaborate on your thoughts below:

_____

_____

_____

CHAPTER 9

DEATH AND DYING

DEATH AND DYING

"You never want to think of the day that a loved one passes away. Yet, we know that this is one of the guarantees in life."

Olivia L Baylor, LCPC, NCC, DCC

Losing a loved one is not an easy task by any means. When we do lose someone, we experience grief and loss as stated by Elizabeth Kubler Ross.[15] There are many stages to grief and loss. They include denial, anger, bargaining, depression and acceptance. [16] [17] With these stages, partner(s) can have struggles with adjustments and understanding. In a relationship, we know that death can be a very difficult topic. We never want to think of our loved one passing away. Many couples never really know how their partner(s) will want their life to progress once they pass. Completing a legal document or a WILL should be something that is immediately done as a couple once you're married or considering marriage. When you complete a WILL, you

---

[15] Kübler-Ross, E. (1969) *On Death and Dying*, Routledge, ISBN 0-415-04015-9
[16] Kübler-Ross, E. (1969) *On Death and Dying*, Routledge, ISBN 0-415-04015-9
[17] Kübler-Ross, E. (2005) *On Grief and Grieving: Finding the Meaning of Grief Through the Five Stages of Loss*, Simon & Schuster Ltd, ISBN 0-7432-6344-8

should think of the current moment as well as the future. Most legal advisors will suggest a review of your WILL once a year.

As a part of your premarital preparation, I have some clients write a letter to their partner(s) when they update the WILL. This letter speaks to your partner(s) from your current, happier place. One thing that is constantly mentioned in sessions is that they didn't know what their partner thought of them during the time of their death. Partner(s) sometime hold onto that one last conversation. The responsibility of preparing and planning for a partner(s) funeral can become overwhelming, especially when you're trying to simultaneously mourn the loss of your loved one. Use these worksheets to provide some closure to your partner(s) during their time of loss.

GRIEF AND LOSS WORKSHEET

Directions: Review the questions below. Complete the worksheets separately and then review the information together. Use the information below to help you with writing your letter to your partner(s).

When was the first time that you met your partner(s)? _____

What were some of the obstacles that you endured? _____

What are 5 memorable times with your partner(s)?

    1.

    2.

    3.

    4.

    5.

Describe the love and affection for your partner(s)

_____

_____

What do you want your partner(s) to feel after your passing?

_____

_____

Elaborate on your thoughts below:

_____

_____

WILL ATTACHMENT TEMPLATE

Directions: Read the template closely. Complete this worksheet separately, then take time this evening or this week to discuss your answers.

Dear_____,

I wanted to write this letter to you to remind you of who I am in my current state. I want you to know that I love you and cherish the time that we've had together. I remember when we first met on___. Like many couples we experienced some hard times in our relationship(s). Such as:

_____

_____

_____

Yet, we also experienced the memories that I hold dear to my heart throughout our relationship together. Some of those memories include:

_____

_____

_____

_____

I continue to have love and affection for you as my partner(s). As I see my partner as:

_____

_____

_____

After I am no longer alive, I only want for you to feel:_____

I have taken care of everything so that you may continue to cherish our time as partner(s) and not worry.

Love your partner forever,

_____

DO NOT RESUSCITATE (DNR) WORKSHEET

Directions: Review the worksheet below. Include your wants and needs with do not resuscitate (DNR). This should not be used in absence of a complete DNR.

When I am in the following health state I do not wish to be resuscitated:

1.

2.

3.

4.

5.

6.

As my partner(s), I hope that you'll abide and respect my needs.

Signed

_____

STEPS TO GRIEF AND LOSS

Directions: Review the steps to grief and loss so that you're able to better understand any obstacles that your partner(s) may run into after your passing.

1. Denial
2. Anger
3. Bargaining
4. Depression
5. Acceptance[18][19]

Overt time you can accept the loss of a loved one.

---

[18] Kübler-Ross, E. (1969) *On Death and Dying*, Routledge, ISBN 0-415-04015-9

[19] Kübler-Ross, E. (2005) *On Grief and Grieving: Finding the Meaning of Grief Through the Five Stages of Loss*, Simon & Schuster Ltd, ISBN 0-7432-6344-8

WILL REVIEW WORKSHEET

Directions: Review the questions below. Complete the worksheets separately and then review the information together. This is a brief WILL review and not a legal WILL. Use these topics and issues when meeting with an attorney.

What is the amount of outstanding debt that you have? _____

Do you have enough insurance available to cover this debt? _____

If not, have you thought of getting extra insurance? _____

If so, list your insurance provider(s). Include your account number and the phone number to the facility:

Insurance Account Holder	Coverage Amount	Account Number	Insurance Phone Number	Online password and log in information

©Olivia L Baylor LCPC, NCC, DCC

Do you have any property? _____

If so where? _____

Who do you want to leave your property to? _____

If that person does not survive, who do you want to leave the property/taxes to? _____

Include your information below for your partner(s) to review.

Property Address	Mortgage Holder/ Amount Due	Account Number	Mortgage Phone Number	Online password and log in information

Elaborate on your thoughts below:

_____

_____

FUNERAL WORKSHEET

Directions: Read the questions closely. Complete this worksheet separately, then take time this evening or this week to discuss your answers together.

Do you want to be cremated or buried?

_____

Do you have any special requests for your cremation or burial?

_____

Do you want your body to be donated to science?

_____

Do you want a funeral ceremony?

_____

If you answered no, skip the rest of the questions.

Is there any particular funeral home you would like to prepare and bury you?

_____

Is there any particular song or type of music that you want to be played at your funeral?

_____

Is there anyone that you would not want at your funeral service?

_____

Is there anyone that you definitely want at your funeral service?

_____

Do you have any religious needs/requests that must be observed?

_____

Do you want your ceremony to be religious?

_____

Elaborate on your thoughts below:

_____

_____

CHAPTER 10
SECOND MARRIAGES

SECOND MARRIAGES

"The relationship you had before should now be a distant past. Do not let that relationship define or hinder this one."

Olivia L Baylor, LCPC, NCC, DCC

In 2015, there were over 2 million marriages conducted in the United States. [20] Of those number of individuals, in the same time frame, over 800,000 got divorced.[21] Second marriages allow for us to look at our relationship in a unique way as most individuals don't realize it's a second chance at happiness. When getting married for a second, third, fourth, or more time; you have to always look at what caused the previous relationship to end. You need to always self-examine yourself and understand what your role was in the marriage or relationship ending. This type of awareness is important and required to fully understand the impact of the ended or failed past relationship(s) on your life. This is necessary so that your corresponding relationship(s) don't deal with a backlash of issues from your previous ones. Essentially you don't want to blame your current partner(s) for something that

---

[20] *CDC/NCHS National Vital Statistics System(2015). Detailed State Tables. Obtained from https://www.cdc.gov/nchs/data/dvs/national_marriage_divorce_rates_00-15.pdf on October 4, 2017

[21] *CDC/NCHS National Vital Statistics System(2015). Detailed State Tables. Obtained from https://www.cdc.gov/nchs/data/dvs/national_marriage_divorce_rates_00-15.pdf on October 4, 2017

they've not done. For example, if you were cheated on by your previous partner(s) and are now suspicious of your current partner(s)? Do you check their phone when they're not in the room? Do you check their bank statements for what they've spent money on? Even though they haven't done anything wrong, you still don't trust them. Take the time to communicate to your partner(s) about past relationships and how it's affected you. Doing so will save any issues or conflict from your past into your current relationship.

SECOND MARRIAGES WORKSHEET

Directions: Read the questions closely. Complete this worksheet separately, then take time this evening or this week to discuss your answers.

How many times have you been married?

_____

Why did your previous marriage(s) end?

_____

_____

Do you still believe in the notion of marriage?

_____

Do you believe you have to be married?

_____

_____

If you were married before, are you over the relationship?

_____

_____

What about your current partner(s) makes you want to marry them?

_____

_____

What if your partner(s) didn't want to get married?

_____

_____

Do you have closure over your previous marriage/unity and relationship(s)?

_____

If no, why not?

_____

Elaborate on your thoughts below:

_____

_____

SELF EVALUATION WORKSHEET

Directions: Read the questions closely. Complete this worksheet separately, then take time this evening or this week to discuss your answers.

Dear *(Insert your name here)*,

I was previously married or in a unified/polyamory relationship(s) with: _____. I was at fault in that/those relationships because I:

1.

2.

3.

4.

5.

I will work on myself to make sure that I don't transfer any faults or guilt to my new partner(s) by evaluating my fault in the relationship(s). I will continue to evaluate myself in our relationship and I do so openly and willingly.

Signed

_____

VOW TO PARTNER WORKSHEET

Directions: Read the questions closely. Complete this worksheet separately, then take time this evening or this week to discuss your answers.

Dear *(Insert your partner(s) name here)*,

I vow in my relationship to not use my previous relationship issues in my current relationship. Those issues include:

1.
2.
3.
4.
5.

I vow to see that my partner(s) is not at fault for my wrongdoings, my ex's wrongdoings, or notions that I have not discussed before. I promise that once I see those issues arise in my mind through behaviors such as suspicion, negative self-talk, or irrational beliefs that I will come to you (insert partner(s) name) and communicate about it. I make this vow to you today (insert partner(s) name) as my everlasting promise.

Signed

_____

©Olivia L Baylor LCPC, NCC, DCC

CHAPTER 11
POLYAMORY PARTNER(S)

POLYAMORY PARTNER(S)

"Love can include one person or multiple partner(s). No matter how you view it, it's still love."

Olivia L Baylor, LCPC, NCC, DCC

When you have enough love for one another and want to show your love with different people, you may be involved in a polyamorous relationship(s). Some individuals within the U.S. culture may see this as taboo. However, polyamorous relationship(s) in other cultures and religions is an acceptable and nonjudgmental form of sharing yourself with another person*. In the United States in 2012, over 3 percent of Americans were in a polyamorous relationship(s).[22] As you prepare for your union or sharing of yourself with someone; you need to know where your place is in that relationship(s). In all relationships, it's important to have an agreement, a clear understanding of standards and in some cases, a written statement of what you expect. This information allows for partner(s) to fully understand their place in the relationship(s). Consider if your partner(s) began to date another partner(s)? Have you talked about what you want to know in their relationship(s)? Have you discussed how you want to introduce yourself to your partner(s) parents?

---

[22] Schucart, B. (Jan 08, 2016) Polyamory by the numbers. www.Advocate.com on October 4, 2017

Do you want your extended family in your relationship(s)? Do you want a cellular family in the future? These are all the questions to consider when going into a relationship(s) so that issues do not later arise.

POLYAMORY AGREEMENT WORKSHEET

Directions: Read the questions closely. Complete this worksheet separately, then take time this evening or this week to discuss your answers.

On nights when you are together with your primary partner, do you want to allow time for any other partner(s)? _____

Do you want your partner to engage in body fluid monogamy? _____

Are you into Candaulism? _____

Does your partner have any needs that you feel like you cannot deliver on?
_____

What night(s) do you expect to be with your partner(s)?
_____

What night(s) do you expect to have alone?
_____

Can your partner(s) communicate with one another on their designated night with you?
_____

©Olivia L Baylor LCPC, NCC, DCC

How do you think your financial responsibilities should be divided?

_____

_____

How do you feel you and your partner(s) should communicate to your children about your relationship?

_____

_____

How do you feel you and your partner(s) should communicate to your parents/ family about your relationship?

_____

_____

Do you have any reservations for bringing more partner(s) into your relationship?

_____

_____

Do you have a point where you feel your relationship with your partner(s) has gone too far sexually?

_____

_____

Do you want to have a recommitment ceremony whenever you bring a partner(s) into your lives?

_____

_____

Elaborate on your thoughts below:

_____

_____

POLYAMORY INTIMACY/SEX AGREEMENT WORKSHEET

Directions: Read the questions closely. Complete this worksheet separately, then take time this evening or this week to discuss your answers.

We agree to abide by the rules within our relationships as partners.

When considering intimacy with one of our partner(s) we agree to:

_____

_____

When it comes to sexual protection with our partner(s) we agree to:

_____

_____

When it comes to kissing our partner(s) we agree to:

_____

_____

When it comes to choosing a partner(s) for ourselves or for one another we agree to:

_____

_____

I'm okay with my partner(s) engaging in sexual activity which includes:

_____

_____

I'm not okay with my partner(s) engaging in sexual activity which includes:

_____

_____

We do this out of respect for our relationship(s) and for one another.

Signed

_____

POLYAMORY TIME AGREEMENT WORKSHEET

Directions: Read the agreement closely and sign. Complete this worksheet separately, then take time this evening or this week to discuss your answers.

We agree to abide by the rules within our relationship(s) as partner(s). When we're spending time together, we agree, to allow for extra time for each partner so there is individual love given. We agree to communicate to our partner(s) when we feel as though we're not receiving our individual time needed. We agree not to conduct malicious behavior, lie, or cheat on our partner(s). We agree to give each other the necessary time for each other and respect when we have time with our partner(s) individually. We do this for the love of each other.

Signed

_____

CHOOSING PARTNER WORKSHEET

Directions: Review the worksheet below and sign. Complete this worksheet separately, then take time this evening or this week to discuss your answers.

I would like for our next partner to have_____.

If age matters, I'd like our next partner to be_____. I want someone who believes in the polyamorous principles within our relationship. In order to do that, I am against/for (circle one) the person to be someone who has been poly in their lifestyle. I agree to openly experience this new relationship energy for myself and my partner(s). I agree that if the person is not meeting the needs of our relationship(s), that we will remove the person from our lives.

Signed

_____

©Olivia L Baylor LCPC, NCC, DCC

POLYAMORY TERMS WORKSHEET

DEFINITIONS:

Body Fluid Monogamy

"The practice of limiting any activity which involves the exchange of bodily fluids, including such activities as unprotected sexual intercourse, to only one partner."[23]

Candaulism

"Sexual arousal from watching one's spouse have sex with or engage in sexual activity with another person."[24]

---

[23] More Than Two: Franklin Veaux's polyamory site. Obtained from https://www.morethantwo.com/polyglossary.html on October 4, 2017

[24] More Than Two: Franklin Veaux's polyamory site. Obtained from https://www.morethantwo.com/polyglossary.html on October 4, 2017

HAND FASTING CEREMONY POEM

On this day we become one

As we bind our hands.

You take my right hand, as I take your left hand.

Making them one.

These ropes we bind in many colors to show and share our love.

I give you my heart, my love my understanding.

My ears to listen when you need to talk.

My tears when you are hurt

My patience when you are running late

I would give you the world, but as you can see. I have given you all of me.

As this rope is a symbol of my love for you.

Let no one cut this rope, for we are now one. I give you my soul, my heart, for we shall never part.

Will you be mine?

By: Evelyn Linton

View more poems by Evelyn Linton by going to www.sunshine.weebly.com

CHAPTER 12

DISABILITIES/ ILLNESSES

DISABILITIES/ILLNESSES

"You should be able to love your partner after their disability/illness, the same way you loved them before."

Olivia L Baylor, LCPC, NCC, DCC

This topic tends to be a non-conventional topic in pre-marital counseling. However, disabilities and illnesses can happen at any time in a relationship. It can happen to your children, to your friends, and family members. Due to the emotional stress, financial stress, and lack of wanting to get help, some couples turn away from their spouse and choose to divorce. Some issues that result from the changes include struggling with anger, regret, new compromises, and feelings of loneliness.[25] Other topics include not wanting to engage in treatment or take medication. As a partner(s) of someone struggling with illness or disability it can be difficult to adjust and cope with changes. You sometimes wonder if the relationship is worth it. However, you need to remember that this is the same person you married or united yourself with, but with new struggles. You have to remember why you love them? Ask yourself why you wanted to be with them? This doesn't take into the account that your spouse has changed. Just remembering why you're with them can sometimes help you through this struggling time.

---

[25] Parker, G. (1993). Disability, caring and marriage: the experience of younger couples when a partner is disabled after marriage. *The British Journal of Social Work, 23*(6), 565-580.

DISABILITY/ILLNESS WORKSHEET

Directions: Review the worksheet below. Include your letter to your partner(s) as a remembrance of yourself in this stage that you're in.

Dear (Insert Partners Name Here),

As you can see I'm not my usual self. I want you to remember me as I am.

When we first met, you described me as_____. You thought

that I was always_____. You said my best qualities were

_____. You always laughed whenever I_____.

You always saw me as a_____. Now that I'm in this state, I

want you to always remember me as I am. If I have caused you pain I

apologize. I love (you/both/all)

Always,

_____

©Olivia L Baylor LCPC, NCC, DCC

COPING SKILLS WORKSHEET

Directions: Review the worksheet below. Include some of your coping skills that work for you. Take the time this evening or this week to review your answers.

When I'm stressed, I display the following *physical signs* :

_____

_____

When I'm stressed, I display the following *emotional signs* :

_____

_____

Some ways that I can cope with my stress include:

_____

_____

When I'm worried, I display the following *physical signs* :

_____

_____

When I'm worried, I display the following *emotional signs*:

_____

_____

Some ways that I can cope when I'm worried include:

_____

_____

When I'm angry, I display the following *physical signs*:

_____

_____

When I'm angry, I display the following *emotional signs*:

_____

_____

Some ways that I can cope with my anger include:

_____

_____

When I'm overwhelmed, I display the following *physical signs* :

_____

_____

When I'm overwhelmed, I display the following *emotional signs*:

_____

_____

Some ways that I can cope with me being overwhelmed include:

_____

_____

Elaborate on your thoughts below:

_____

_____

COPING SKILLS ACTIVITIES WORKSHEET

Directions: Review the worksheet below. Include some of your coping skills that work for you.

Some **no-cost** activities that I love to do include:

1.

2.

3.

4.

5.

Some **low-cost** activities that I love to do include:

1.

2.

3.

4.

5.

©Olivia L Baylor LCPC, NCC, DCC

Some activities that I've never ever done, but want to do include:

1.

2.

3.

4.

5.

Elaborate on your thoughts below:

_____

_____

CHAPTER 13
PERSONAL SPACE/QUALITY TIME

PERSONAL SPACE/QUALITY TIME

"You should still be you, even though you are now married."

Olivia L Baylor, LCPC, NCC, DCC

Personal space in a marriage can allow for your partner(s) to feel as though they're still their same individual self. When you get married many partner(s) tend to blend marriage time and individual time together. When you do this, they begin lose themselves in their marriage. When this occurs, some people can become resentful, angry, or distant towards their partner(s). Some partner(s) may struggle with the feeling as though their partner(s) don't connect with them on the things they enjoy in life. They may feel as though their partner(s) don't know them anymore. However, that's not the always the case.

I'm here to say it's okay that your partner(s) doesn't like or have an interest in *everything* that you do. Imagine if you and your partner(s) had the same exact interests, you'd basically be marrying yourself. This doesn't mean that you don't try to find ways to connect to one another. You can still give your partner(s) quality time by engaging in activities that you both enjoy, as well as creating new activities together. It's important to remember to allow individual time to your partner(s) around your activities. For example, let's say you're about to watch the football game and your partner(s) not interested. Maybe take your partner(s) out to lunch before the game to have quality time together. Then enjoy having your individual time for your own personal enjoyment. Again, **personal space is fine as long as it doesn't impede on quality time together**. You need to have both in order to not feel as though your relationship is based off of time *always* together versus time apart. In a marriage/unity, this is what is known as *compromise.*

PERSONAL SPACE WORKSHEET

Directions: Review the worksheet below. Include your wants and needs with personal space and sign for your partner(s).

I vow, to give personal space to my partner(s) whenever they need it. This time should not impede on our quality time together. Some things that I know my partner(s) likes to do with their personal time include:

_____

_____

Some things that I like to do when we are together include:

_____

_____

I vow to try my best to not get angry with their quality time or our relationship. I promise to try not to engage in self-blame, self-guilt, obsessive thoughts or negative self-talk regarding my partner(s) time.

Signed

_____

SHARED ACTIVITY WORKSHEET

Directions: Review the worksheet below. Include some shared activities that you and your partner(s) can engage in.

Some activities that I feel I can engage in with my partner(s) include:

1.

2.

3.

4.

5.

6.

7.

8.

9.

10.

QUALITY TIME ACTIVITY

Directions: Review the activity below. Try to engage in these activities whenever you feel as though your relationship is becoming stagnant.

Activity:

Make a list of 5 activities (preferably low or no cost) that you've each always wanted to do, have done or enjoy. Take a hat and place all of the activities in the hat. Once a week, month or whenever you need, pick the activity from the hat and complete it.

Rules:

You may not sneak later and take your partner(s) activity out of the hat.

You may not say I do not want to engage in the activity.

No dangerous or activities that you know your partner(s) will dislike. This is to bring you together not pull you apart.

You must take turns.

CHAPTER 14

INTERRACIAL RELATIONSHIPS

INTERRACIAL RELATIONSHIPS

"You may love your partner(s) for who they are, and not the color of their skin. Yet, you still have to acknowledge the differences between the two."

Olivia L Baylor, LCPC, NCC, DCC

Loving someone from another race or culture can blossom into a beautiful melting pot. However, it's important to note the differences between you and your partner(s) race. An example may include different upbringings, beliefs, and cultural rituals. You may also encounter issues with what others think or believe about your relationship(s), which can be a hindrance within it. Have you thought about your own internal racism? Be mindful of the historical context within your relationship and how that can cause bias and discrimination from others. You have to also consider those "other individuals" may include family members and close friends. There's numerous factors and issues to discuss on how you feel regarding this and your expectations for your relationship. Review the worksheets attached regarding interracial relationships. Take the time to communicate amongst yourself, as well as with your friends & family.

INTERRACIAL RELATIONSHIP WORKSHEET

Directions: Read the agreement closely and sign. Complete this worksheet separately, then take time this evening or this week to discuss your thoughts.

What would you do if your child(ren) decides to marry a person from another race?

_____

_____

Does race in a relationship matter? _____

Why or why not?

_____

_____

Have you felt as though your partner(s), family, friends, and co-workers treat you a certain way because of your race?

_____

_____

©Olivia L Baylor LCPC, NCC, DCC

How do you feel about being in an interracial relationship?

_____

_____

If your family disapproves of your relationship, how will you handle it?

_____

_____

Do you feel as though your relationship is strong enough to handle racism?

_____

_____

Have you or your partner ever discussed your internal racism?

_____

_____

Elaborate on your thoughts below:

_____

_____

CHAPTER 15

INTERRELIGIOUS RELATIONSHIPS

INTERRELIGIOUS RELATIONSHIPS

"You may call each of your Gods by a different name. However you each believe one thing and that is..... there is one."

Olivia L Baylor, LCPC, NCC, DCC

Interreligious relationships can pull and connect a family together. Depending on the type of religion it can divide partner(s) to consider how their child(ren) will be raised. For example, consider an Orthodox Jewish marriage where the mother is not Jewish. The child(ren) in that case would not be considered Jewish as the child would not have their faith passed down by their mother. [26] How would this affect your relationship with your family? Would your family condemn or disown you for marrying outside of your religion? With all religions, there are differences amongst them that can cause for some couples to communicate about their viewpoint of their God(s) or their spirituality. Does this make your union or marriage any less than other partner(s) marriages? Does it cause a competitive drive over what it means to be the holiest/religious? Or does it begin a process of allowing you to see that your marriage is in need of guidance in your union? When we speak of

---
[26] Adar, Rabbi Ruth. "Can a Person Be 'Half Jewish'?" *ReformJudaism.org*, 21 Mar. 2014, reformjudaism.org/blog/2013/10/07/can-person-be-half-jewish.

religion we need to know what our partner(s) beliefs are. Do they align together? Are they against one another? When you have child(ren), would their religious choices be an issue? Let's look into this closer by reviewing the worksheet to see where there are some topics that need to be explored.

INTERRELIGIOUS RELATIONSHIP WORKSHEET

Directions: Read the agreement closely and sign. Complete this worksheet separately, then take time this evening or this week to discuss your thoughts.

Is religion important to you?_____ If not/so, why?

_____

_____

Do you expect your partner(s) to believe in God, be spiritual or believe in a higher power?

_____

Does your partner(s) believe in God, is spiritual or has belief of a higher power?

_____

What do you want your child(ren) to believe when they get older?

_____

_____

Do you expect your partner(s) to convert to your religion/beliefs?

_____

Do you want religious practices as a part of your wedding? _____

Do you want religious practices as a part of your funeral? _____

Do you expect your child(ren) to be circumcised?

_____

How do you expect to celebrate the holidays?

_____

_____

(For Step-Parents) If your partner(s) child(ren) spends holidays with their other family; how do you feel about them following their religious beliefs?

_____

_____

Elaborate on your thoughts below:

_____

_____

CHAPTER 16
STEP-CHILDREN

STEP-CHILDREN

"Even though they may not be related to you by blood, they can still be your child(ren)."

Olivia L Baylor, LCPC, NCC, DCC

When you have a step-child(ren) it can be difficult for them to understand your role in their lives. This can be a challenge that you may face when interacting with your step-child(ren). Some partner(s) may have a difficult time with creating a bond within the relationship. Bonds are necessary in order for the child(ren) to feel as though they can be connected to you. Once division is created, the child(ren) will believe that the only person they're connected to is their parent(s) and not the step-parent. Think of this situation from the child(ren)'s perspective. Why then should they respect or acknowledge you? Do you think dislike from your step-child(ren) can cause relationship issues? Here's an easy answer, yes it can and it will. Does that mean you will make your partner choose? Or will you leave? Before making any rash decisions, imagine how the child(ren) is feeling. A new person is now taking the role of my previous parent. Consider how your step-child(ren) is dealing with the issue at hand. The first step in building a relationship with your step-child(ren) is trying to connect with them. Once you find ways to connect with your step-child(ren), you can build more than just a bond, but a family.

STEP-CHILDREN WORKSHEET

Directions: Read the questions closely. Complete this worksheet separately, then take time this evening or this week to discuss your answers.

Do you want your step-child(ren) to call you by a particular name and/or pronoun?

_____

Do you feel as though your partner(s) understands your relationship with **YOUR** child(ren)?

_____

Do you feel as though you should be the primary person to discipline the child(ren)?

_____

How do you feel about your partner(s) step-child(ren)?

_____

_____

Do you have a relationship with **YOUR** step-child(ren)/child(ren)?

_____

Do you want more of a relationship with **YOUR** step-child(ren)/child(ren)?

_____

Do you feel as though you understand your role in the life of your step-child(ren)?
_____

If so, what is your role?

_____

_____

If no, what do you want your role to be?

_____

_____

What does co-parenting look like for you as the non-biological step parent?

_____

_____

What does co-parenting look like for you as the biological parent?

_____

_____

©Olivia L Baylor LCPC, NCC, DCC

How do you expect to spend the holidays with your step-child(ren)?

_____

_____

Are you okay with engaging with your partner(s) exes, their child(ren) and their family during the holidays?

_____

_____

Are you okay with your partner(s) engaging with their exes, their exes children and their family during the holidays?

_____

_____

Elaborate on your thoughts below:

_____

_____

CHAPTER 17
INFERTILITY/PMAD

INFERTILITY/PMAD

"If your partner(s) can't reproduce will you still stay? Can you see the signs of PMAD and know how to help your partner?"

Olivia L Baylor, LCPC, NCC, DCC

Some couples struggle with the physically birthing of their child(ren). Some couples also deal with sudden loss of a child(ren). When these struggles occur, some individuals wonder if it's a problem within the relationship and not a medical condition. With loss and the struggle of pregnancy, some individuals can deal with confusion, anger, regret, depression, and sometimes, Post Traumatic Stress Disorder (PTSD). How do you help your partner(s) when they feel this way? Being aware of your partner(s) signs and their health can be vital during this time.

Some individuals struggle with infant loss and traumatic birth, which can lead to postpartum mood and anxiety disorder (PMAD). When this happens, some relationships struggle to stay together. According to Mothers Strong, "1 in 7 women suffer from postpartum depression and anxiety.[27]" Being an effective partner(s) who listens and knows when their partner(s) is in need is important.

---

[27] Mothers Strong. Innovative Community Solutions. https://static1.squarespace.com/static/56d5ca187da24ffed7378b40/t/59b968067e7b58305ea8dbb7/1505323025577/Innovative+Community+Solutions+Mothers+Strong+Butte+County-MMH+Innovation+Awards.pdf obtained on October 6, 2017.

Effective listening in a relationship includes listening to your partner(s) verbal and nonverbal cues. In relation to PMAD, some of the cues are verbal and some of the cues are nonverbal. Sometimes it's harder to decipher which one is which. Review the attached worksheets and review some of the nonverbal and verbal cues to consider when interacting with your partner after a childbirth, infertility or child(ren) loss. As you will see below, I've provided worksheets on explaining a need for support from friends and family members during this time, along with a poem written by someone who has also experienced a loss.

PMAD WORKSHEET

Direction: Read the cues below. Keep them in a safe space to review.

Verbal Cues	Nonverbal cues
I'm hurt	Moping around
I'm sad	Withdrawn from others
I feel lost	Excessive crying
I don't know myself	Spontaneous crying
Help me	Excessive/No sleeping
I need you	Lack/ increase in eating
I should just go away	Excessive weight loss/gain

Add cues that are missing below:

_____   _____

_____   _____

_____   _____

PMAD LETTER TEMPLATE

Directions: Review the template closely. Complete this worksheet separately, then take time this evening or this week to discuss your answers.

Dear (Insert Visitors Name Here),

As you can see we have just had a baby. I know this is a joyous moment in not just our lives together, but in the life that we share as a family. I want to thank you for being a part of this moment for me. I now want to ask you to please help us. I know you're excited to hold our child(ren); we are excited for you. The help that you give us at this time will allow for us to rest, heal, and prepare to continue the journey of being loving parent(s). We ask that when you come over to please take one of the tasks below and complete them. Once completed we ask that you then take our child(ren) and have your time with them. We thank you for being able to consider this for us and to be there for us as we work to try to find time for rest and being the best parent(s) we can be.

Love,

_____

PMAD CLEANING/HELP TEMPLATE

Directions: Review the worksheet below. Check off the items needed for help from family members while they're in your home.

Rooms	Week 1	Initial	Week 2	Initial	Week 3	Initial	Week 4	Initial
Bathroom								
Living room								
Kitchen								
Bedroom								
Dining room								

Remember to keep track of the family members who have provided help to you. When you're up for it, send them thank you letters as a gesture of your appreciation of them being there for you.

©Olivia L Baylor LCPC, NCC, DCC

THANK YOU LETTER TRACKING SHEET

Directions: Review the worksheet below. Complete it when family and friends come to your home.

Name	Item Completed	Date Completed	Thank you sent?
Cousin Lucy	*Vacuumed*	*09/28/2015*	*Yes*

THANK YOU LETTER TEMPLATE

Directions: Review the worksheet below. Complete it when family and friends come to your home.

Dear (Insert Visitors Name Here),

Thank you for taking the time to come to my house on _____ and _____. I appreciate all of the hard work, time, and effort that you put into the helping us. You being there for us means more than you know. Thank you again.

Love,

_____

YOU ARE NOT AT FAULT POEM

I must let you go

I think of you every day, the way you fell within, so small so sweet my little one.

I never got to name you, or to hold you close to my heart. I never got to smell you or kiss your little face.

When you closed your eyes to me and took your last breath. I wanted to go with you.

There is a hole in my heart that will never be filled, you took a part of me when you closed your eyes to me.

My tears have started to fall as you lay so quiet and still. My arm reaches out to you just wanting to hold you near. Just to say I love you one last time in your ear. There goes another tear as it falls on your face. If only I could wake you up and put you back in this place.

Truth to be told we will meet again in a place of love and warmth where everyone are friends.

Sleep well my little one, we love you so. Its time for me to say goodbye though I don't want to let you go.

My tears are falling heavily now as I walk out the door. I never will forget you in my heart you will always be.

And when I see the morning light I know you are smiling at me.

(To September you are always in my heart)

By: Evelyn Linton

View more poems by Evelyn Linton by going to www.sunshine.weebly.com

CHAPTER 18

IN-LAWS

IN-LAWS

"Do you really know how your parents feel about your partner(s)? Do you really know how your partner(s) feels about your parent(s)?"

Olivia L Baylor, LCPC, NCC, DCC

In-laws come in many different forms. We have the in-laws who are open and accepting; The in-laws who are withdrawn; The in-laws who discuss immediate disapproval; and in some cases, individuals who don't have parents to share with their partner(s). When your parents dislike your partner(s), it's usually not kept secret. When you consider combining a relationship together, you have to remember your in-laws. Some partner(s) struggle with family conflict, but never discuss how the conflict could've been avoided. Have you ever tried connecting with your in-laws prior to your relationship? Have you looked at how you're marrying their child changed their role in their lives? Have you tried to connect with their rituals, customs, and beliefs? When was the last time you went out individually with them? If these questions really have you wondering then you know you didn't put in the effort. You also know that they didn't as well. So, imagine how your partner(s) feels being in the middle of this? Review the worksheets then communicate on connecting with your in-laws.

IN-LAWS WORKSHEET

Directions: Read the questions closely. Complete this worksheet separately, then take time this evening or this week to discuss your answers.

Do you have any conflict with your in-laws?
_____

Do you really know your in-laws?
_____

How do you feel about your in-laws?
_____
_____
_____

Do you feel as though your parents connect with your partner(s)?
_____

Do you feel as though you connect with your family?
_____

Have you ever put in the effort to connect with your in-laws?
_____

If yes, what have you done?

_____

If no, why not?

_____

If you could change one thing about your partner(s) parental figures(s) what would it be?

_____

_____

_____

Elaborate on your thoughts below:

_____

_____

_____

IN-LAWS ACTIVITY

Directions: Review the activity below. Complete the activity individually. Once complete discuss your outing with your partner(s).

Activity:

Individually take your in-laws out on an activity or dinner. This activity doesn't include your partner(s), only you. You must also complete this activity with each parental figure individually. When you do go out review the questions on the next page as ice breakers to work on your relationship. If you're unable to go out due to distance etc., still ask them these questions to build an individual relationship with them.

IN-LAWS WORKSHEET

Directions: Review the worksheet below. Complete the questions with your in-laws during the activity. Discuss the findings with your partner(s).

What is something you can tell me about your child?

What is the fondest memory that you have with my partner(s)?

Tell me how my partner(s) was as a child or whenever they were in your care.

Is there anything about my relationship with your child that you dislike?

How can our relationship be more productive or stronger?

What's one statement of advice you can give me about my partner(s)?

What's one statement of advice you can give me about our relationship?

What's one statement of advice you can give me about marriage?

What else do you need or want from me?

CHAPTER 19
COMMUNICATION

COMMUNICATION

"Listen to your partner(s), you say you hear them but you're not listening."

Olivia L Baylor, LCPC, NCC, DCC

In a marriage there can be many issues that can arise. Marriage and spouses continue to have issues with communication. [28] When communication is an issue in a relationship it can quickly deteriorate. Communication now comes in different forms with the new age of media. Verbal communication has decreased with the increase of new media usage. Communication now largely consists of text messages and video-based messaging. How does this impact communication? It drastically changes it. For example, consider talking to your partner(s) via text messages. How many times have them misinterpreted what you have said as hostile or confusing? Do arguments arise from the text messages? Do you **assume** that they're blowing things out of proportion? Do different thoughts come through your mind after getting the text? What about simply talking to them face to face and listening? Do you feel awkward with eye contact?

Sometimes you have to listen then repeat what your partner has stated. In counseling there are certain communication techniques known as

---

[28] *Bradbury, Thomas N. *The Developmental Course of Marital Dysfunction*. Cambridge University Press, 2006.

summarizing.[29] This is similar to summarizing a paragraph or statement. However, in an argument you do not always summarize. Partner(s) simply either:

1. *Take a one-word sentence and highly rely on it for verification of why **your** point is correct.*
2. *Talk over your partner to the point where they don't/can't respond.*
3. *Give them the silent treatment and walk away.*

In all three cases you didn't listen to your partner(s). Let's look at some skills or techniques to use with your partner(s).

---

[29] Gerig, M. S. (2018). *Foundations for clinical mental health counseling: an introduction to the profession.* NY, NY: Pearson.

COMMUNICATION COPING SKILLS

Directions: Review the coping skills below. Practice them with your partner(s) during a disagreement.

Walk away and take 5 minutes to cool down. Then go back to communicating with your partner(s).

Process what is happening before responding.

Close your eyes. Take 10 deep breaths slowly. Then go back to communicating with your partner(s)

Listen to your partner(s), respond and validate their understanding.

What are some other coping skills you can think of?

_____

_____

_____

_____

_____

COMMUNICATION ACTIVITY

Directions: Review the activities below. Try the activity one time a week for the next four weeks to see if there's any improvement in your communication together.

Activity:

Take a simple writing pen in your home. Go to your partner(s) when you want to discuss an important matter. Take turns using the pen as the determining factor for who speaks. For example:

If partner 1 has the pen then partner 2 cannot talk or interrupt the other individual(s) and vice versa.

- *Partner 1 voices their opinion or thought.*
- *Then partner 1 must give partner 2 the pen.*
- *Partner 2 must repeat what partner 1 said or summarize it.*
- *Once partner 2 has validated partners 1 statement then partner 2 can give their reasons on the matter.*
- *This continues until everyone has spoken and been validated on their feelings.*

Rules:

1. You must not take the pen and hide it from your partner(s). Each party should have a time to speak.

2. Keep your statements short as your partner(s) will have to listen and summarize your statements.

3. Don't just repeat to repeat, listen to how your partner(s) is/are feeling.

4. Don't respond with "that doesn't make sense". Try to understand or ask for clarification.

FAIR FIGHTING RULES

Directions: Review the rules below. Use this as form of communication rules with your partner when you are having a disagreement.

1. Allow your partner(s) to voice their opinion.
2. No yelling, name calling, or cursing.
3. No silent treatment.
4. No walking away after you have made your comment so that you don't hear your partner(s) response.
5. Give eye contact.
6. No transference of guilt/ blame.
7. No using child(ren) against your partner(s).
8. No bringing up old relationship issues to validate your partner(s) behavior.

COMMUNICATION LETTER TEMPLATE

Directions: Review the letter template below. Complete the template as partner(s) with feedback given from each individual. Sign the letter template once completed.

Dear (Insert Partner(s) Name Here),

When we argue I'm now aware of the unhealthy techniques that I use. I vow that starting today I will begin to no longer:

1.

2.

3.

4.

5.

I vow that instead I will:

1.

2.

3.

4.

5.

I have listened to you and know that it makes you feel_____and that makes me feel_____. I promise to make these changes for the improvement of communication within our relationship.

Love,

_____

CHAPTER 20
MILITARY PARTNER(S)

MILITARY PARTNER(S)

"Your partner(s) should be your FAMILY just like the military is your FAMILY."

Olivia L Baylor, LCPC, NCC, DCC

Military couples struggle with individual relationship issues that are different than what civilian couples will experience. For example, some partner(s) struggle with feelings of loneliness, anger, and denial due to long deployments, time apart, and the responsibility of having to be a sole parent. When partner(s) struggle with these issues they sometimes don't know where to seek help. There are many counseling services offered and resources available to military families on military bases, church-based organizations, and military/veteran community organizations. Struggling to feel loved can also be an issue as military partner(s).

You want to be loved by someone who is present to love you. It's sad to say that divorce and infidelity rates are higher within the military community. Some other issues experienced by military families include domestic violence, child abuse, and neglect. Sadly, partner(s) may return very differently than they were when they left due a number of causes such as physical injury, PTSD, loss of limb/limbs, or in the worst cases death of a loved one. In the worksheet for this section, answer how the military has or will impact your relationship. Review back to the other chapters for worksheets that may correlate with other marital issues.

MILITARY FAMILY WORKSHEET

Directions: Read the questions closely. Complete this worksheet separately, then take time this evening or this week to discuss your answers.

What are the things you need from your partner(s) while they are stationed?
_____
_____

What options do you have with maintaining a sexual/intimate relationship while they're away?
_____
_____

What if anything would you change with your communication with your partner(s)?
_____
_____

How do you feel about your partner(s) being in the military?
_____
_____

Has the military impacted your relationship? If so, how?
_____
_____

Elaborate on your responses below:
_____
_____

CHAPTER 21
SUICIDE

SUICIDE

"Suicide is the silent killer that does not give you a warning it just takes your loved one away."

Olivia L Baylor, LCPC, NCC, DCC

Over 40,000 people in 2015 were successful at committing suicide.[30] Some individuals may not always take the time to seek help for their suicidal thoughts. When there's no warning given many family members and friends worry that they missed the signs or didn't do enough for their loved one. Sometimes signs are given, while other times nothing is mentioned. The fault is not on you when this occurs. Let's consider how you can ask your partner(s) about their feelings and thoughts. Do you know your partner(s) family history with suicide? Have they struggled with depression in the past? Have you noticed a change in their behavior? When a person feels as though they want to take their lives, they've reached a point in their life that their existence is no longer needed. Some factors that could increase suicidal thought/attempts include drug usage, mental health issues, previous attempts, traumatic events, medical issues, and surrounding factors within their lives (job loss etc.). In

---

[30] National Institute of Mental Health (2015). Suicide is a leading cause of death in the United States. Retrieved October 6, 2017, from https://www.nimh.nih.gov/health/statistics/suicide/index.shtml#part_153200

2015, out of the over 40,000 individuals who were successful at committing suicide; over 20,000 used firearms, approximately 11,000 were through suffocation, almost 7,000 were through poisoning, and over 3,000 conducted suicide in other methods.[31] There's still a bias in relation to suicidal attempts, in which women attempt suicide at a higher rate than males.[32] However, men are more likely to be successful at committing suicide as they use more lethal means as opposed to women.[33] When you have a family or partner(s) who has suicidal ideation thoughts or depression, there are some methods and techniques to use. Filling out a safety plan as a measure for you to prepare if this does happen to your partner(s). Observe your partner(s) behavior and if you have suspicion or a gut feeling seek a medical professional help immediately or call 911.

---

[31] National Institute of Mental Health (2015). Number of suicide deaths by method. Retrieved October 6, 2017, from https://www.nimh.nih.gov/health/statistics/suicide/index.shtml#part_153201

[32] **National Institute of Mental Health (2015). Number of suicide deaths by method. Retrieved October 6, 2017, from https://www.nimh.nih.gov/health/statistics/suicide/index.shtml#part_153201

[33] **National Institute of Mental Health (2015). Number of suicide deaths by method. Retrieved October 6, 2017, from https://www.nimh.nih.gov/health/statistics/suicide/index.shtml#part_153201

SUICIDE SAFETY PLAN WORKSHEET

Directions: Review the safety plan below. Complete the worksheet separately. Keep this plan in a safe and accessible place in your home. Consider also giving family or friends a copy of this in case of an emergency. This is not a preventive measure to seeking help. If you're having thoughts of suicide seek medical help or dial 911.

Name: _____   Age: _____   DOB: _____

When I am getting thoughts to harm myself, what does that look like:

_____

_____

When I feel as though things are becoming overwhelming I will:

_____

_____

I can cope and calm myself down by:

1.

2.

©Olivia L Baylor LCPC, NCC, DCC

3.

4.

5.

My support system includes: *These are the people you call immediately when you're feeling suicidal.*

Name	Address	Phone Number	Ways they help
Mrs. Paula Paula	*555 Happiness Street*	*410-555-5555*	*Makes me laugh, listens to me*

Places that I can go for safety: *These are the places that you can go to immediately when you're feeling suicidal. At the minimum 2 hospitals should be listed as a referral point.*

Name	Address	Phone Number	EMERGENCY NUMBER
Hospital 1	*555 Happiness Street*	*410-555-5555*	*911*

Medical professionals I can contact: *These are the people that you can contact immediately when you are feeling suicidal.*

Name	Address	Phone Number	CRISIS LINE
Dr. Doctor	*555 Happiness Street*	*410-555-5555*	*410-555-5555*

What needs to be removed from my environment so that I maintain my safety:

1.

2.

3.

4.

5.

Why should I seek help from my family/friends/medical professionals, etc.?

_____

_____

What/Who will I leave behind if I harm myself?

_____

_____

What are the consequences of this choice?

_____

_____

My current medications:

_____

_____

My allergies include:

_____

_____

In what ways will I be missed?

1.

2.

3.

4.

5.

If you are feeling suicidal contact the National Prevention Lifeline at 1-800-273-TALK(8255)

SUICIDE HOTLINE NUMBERS

Please note: This is not a complete list of hotline or services available. Also, I cannot confirm that each number is active and the best option for you. If you have a number of contact that you feel should be added, please contact me via email at baylorbook@gmail.com.

List of Suicide Hotline

Argentina: +5402234930430

Australia: 131114

Austria: 017133374

Belgium: 106

Botswana: 3911270

Brazil: 212339191

Canada: 5147234000 (Montreal); 18662773553 (outside Montreal)

Canada: Trans Lifeline 877-330-6366

China: 85223820000

Croatia: 014833888

Denmark: +4570201201

Egypt: 7621602

Finland: 040-5032199

France: 0145394000

Germany: 08001810771

Holland: 09000767

India: 8888817666

Ireland: +4408457909090

Italy: 800860022

Japan: +810352869090

Mexico: 5255102550

New Zealand: 045861048

Norway: +4781533300

Philippines: 028969191

Poland: 5270000

Russia: 0078202577577

Spain: 914590050

South Africa: 0514445691

Sweden: 46317112400

Switzerland: 143

United Kingdom: 08457909090

United States: Georgia Crisis & Access Line 1800-715-4225

United States: Hopeline (Call or text) 919-231-4525/1877-235-4525

United States: National Suicide Prevention Lifeline 1800-273-TALK(8255)

United States: The Trevor Project 1866-488-7386

United States: Trans Lifeline 1877-565-8860

United States: Veterans Crisis Line 1800-27-8255[34]

---

[34] List of International Suicide Hotlines. (n.d.). Retrieved October 06, 2017, from http://ibpf.org/resource/list-international-suicide-hotlines

CHAPTER 22

SELF ESTEEM

SELF ESTEEM

"Your self-esteem can be perceived as an evaluation of yourself and your partner(s)."

Olivia L Baylor, LCPC, NCC, DCC

Having low self-esteem can be difficult for others to understand. However, there are some factors that increase that belief; it can include achievement in life, looks, relationship status, or happiness. When these factors are included in a marriage or a unification of a relationship(s) it can be difficult for the others to grasp how you feel. Sometimes in a relationship, self-esteem of a partner(s) typically decreases during high traumatic or stressful times such as childbirth, switching jobs, moving, loss of family members, jealousy, comparison of self to others, infidelity on either partner(s) behalf, as well as past traumatic situation. When this does happen, partner(s) should try to see what they can do to help their partner(s) feel more positive about their self and their image. This is when communication and effective listening play a major role in the relationship. What is it that your partner is asking from you? Do they want to see how you react to their new belief of themselves? Do you react negatively and justify their belief? Sometimes low self-esteem can deeply impact a person so much that they consider committing suicide.

Therefore, begin to take the required steps to acknowledge changes in your partner(s) and listen to what your partner(s) is communicating about their needs.

SELF ESTEEM REFERENCE WORKSHEET

*Directions: Write a reference letter to yourself hiring yourself to be **you**. In all reference letters there's no place for negative statements only positive remarks about yourself.*

Dear (Insert YOUR name here),

I am referring (Insert YOUR name here) to be an employee to myself because:

_____

_____

_____

I have the following qualities that allow for me to be vital to myself:

_____

_____

_____

I highly recommend this person to this position.

Signed

_____

HOW I SEE MYSELF WORKSHEET

Directions: Use a list of positive words to describe yourself. Apply your face to this form and consider how you view yourself through your own lenses.

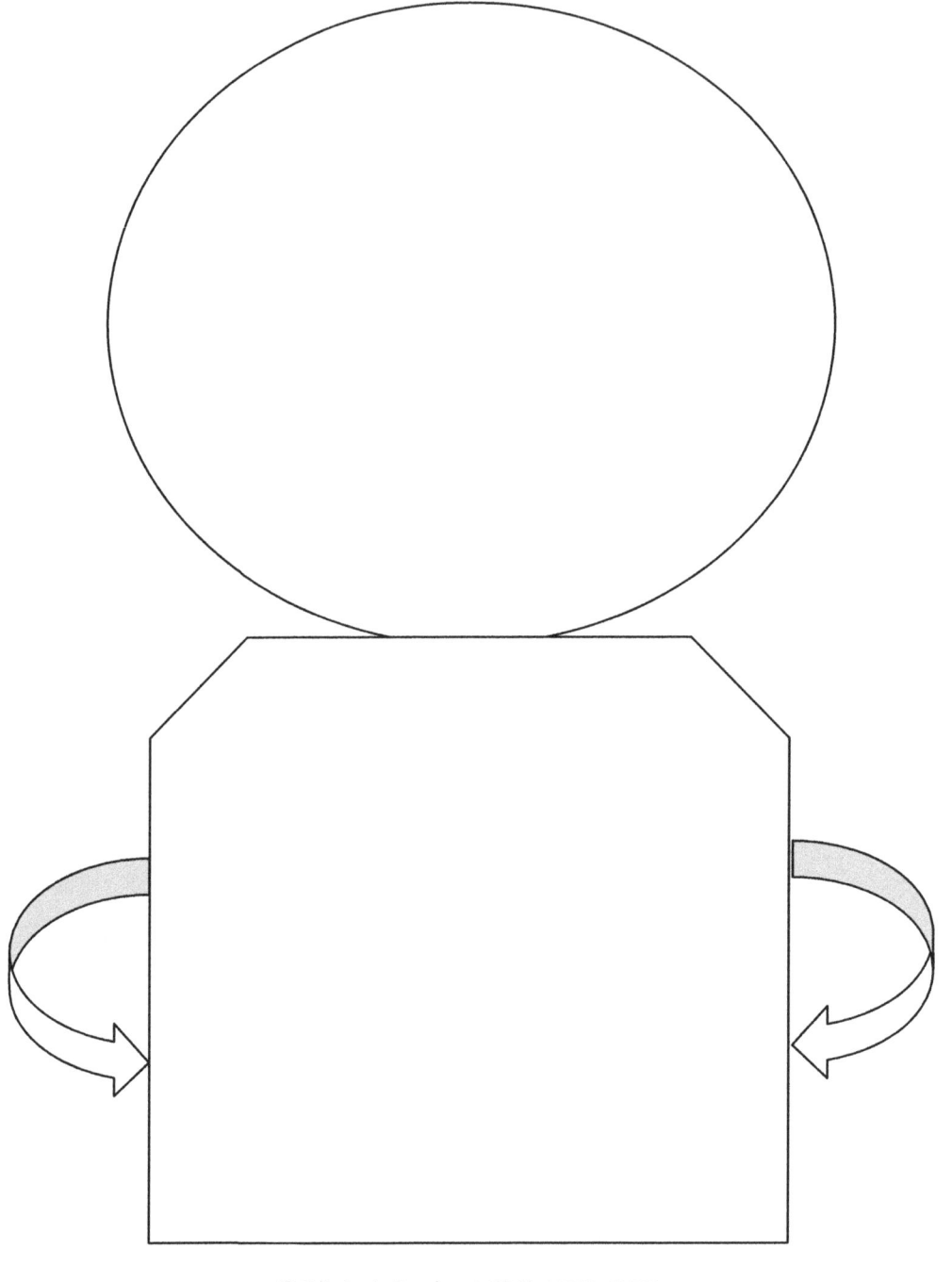

©Olivia L Baylor LCPC, NCC, DCC

MANTRA WORKSHEET

Directions: Complete the worksheet below to create your own mantra to a part of your daily routine. Use this mantra and repeat it to yourself when you're dealing with self-esteem issues.

The mantra that I want to use to describe me and encourage me is:

_____

_____

_____

_____

I will repeat this mantra to myself daily, hourly, or whenever necessary to describe who I am as a person. This promise I make to myself.

Signed

_____

©Olivia L Baylor LCPC, NCC, DCC

CHAPTER 23

DOMESTIC VIOLENCE

DOMESTIC VIOLENCE

"In a relationship there are times that you don't know that your partner(s) behavior is unhealthy. It's when you finally identify that behavior that sometimes it's too late."

Olivia L Baylor, LCPC, NCC, DCC

Domestic violence (DV) can come in different forms in a relationship(s). Sometimes while you're in the relationship you don't identify it as DV, instead you simply assume that your partner(s) is *passionate* about the way that they interact with you. Within DV there are different forms of abuse that can be portrayed by your partner(s). It includes physical abuse, emotional/verbal abuse, sexual abuse, and financial abuse.[35] With the new inclusion of the internet there's also now internet abuse. According to the power and control wheel by the Domestic Abuse Intervention Project,[36] there are some warning signs to the abuse. They include "using coercion and threats; using intimidation, using emotional abuse, using isolation, minimizing, denying and blaming, using children, using male privilege (heterosexual); using privilege

---

[35] Garcia-Moreno, C., AFM Jansen, H., Ellsberg, M., Heise, L. & Watts, C.H., (2006). Prevalence of Intimate Partner Violence: Findings From the WHO Multi-Country Study on Women's Health and Domestic Violence. (2007). *Obstetrics & Gynecology, 109*(1), 198. doi:10.1097/01.aog.0000252267.04622.80

[36] *Pence & Peymar. "Power and Control Wheel." Domestic Abuse Intervention Project, National Center on Domestic and Sexual Violence, 1993,* www.ncdsv.org/publications_wheel.html.

(LGBTQ) and using economic abuse". If you're continuing to experience this abuse in your household you can contact the National Domestic Violence hotline in regards to abusive situations at 1-800-799-7233. Review the power and control wheel now with your partner(s) if you notice any behaviors that you feel like need to be addressed seek professional help.

POWER AND CONTROL WHEEL

Directions: Review the power and control wheel to understand how abuse continues to be a cycle. Communicate with your partner about your findings.

[37]

---

[37] *Pence & Peymar. "Power and Control Wheel." Domestic Abuse Intervention Project, National Center on Domestic and Sexual Violence, 1993,* www.ncdsv.org/publications_wheel.html.

Power and Control Wheel for Lesbian, Gay, Bisexual and Trans Relationships

HETEROSEXISM · HOMOPHOBIA · BIPHOBIA · TRANSPHOBIA

PHYSICAL VIOLENCE · SEXUAL (outer ring behaviors: slapping, pushing, shoving, hitting, tripping, twisting arms, biting, kicking, punching, grabbing, choking, putting hair, gripping)

POWER AND CONTROL

USING COERCION & THREATS
making and/or carrying out threats to do something to harm you • threatening to leave or commit suicide • driving recklessly to frighten you • threatening to "out" you • threatening others who are important to you • stalking

USING INTIMIDATION
making you afraid by using looks, gestures, actions • smashing things • abusing pets • displaying weapons • using looks, actions, gestures to reinforce homophobic, biphobic or transphobic control

USING EMOTIONAL ABUSE
putting you down • making you feel bad about yourself • calling you names • playing mind games • making you feel guilty • humiliating you • questioning if you are a "real" lesbian, "real" man, "real" woman, "real" femme, "real" butch, etc. • reinforcing internalized homophobia, biphobia or transphobia

USING ISOLATION
controlling what you do, who you see or talk to • limiting your outside activities • using jealousy to control you • making you account for your whereabouts • saying no one will believe you, especially not if you are lesbian, gay, bisexual, or trans • not letting you go anywhere alone

DENYING, MINIMIZING, & BLAMING
making light of the abuse • saying it didn't happen • shifting responsibility for abusive behavior • saying it is your fault, you deserved it • accusing you of "mutual abuse" • saying women can't abuse women/ men can't abuse men • saying it's just "fighting," not abuse

USING CHILDREN
making you feel guilty about the children • using children to relay messages • threatening to take the children • threatening to tell your ex-spouse or authorities that you are lesbian, gay, bisexual or trans so they will take the children

USING PRIVILEGE
treating you like a servant • making all the big decisions • being the one to define each partner's roles or duties in the relationship • using privilege or ability to "pass" to discredit you, put you in danger, cut off your access to resources, or use the system against you

USING ECONOMIC ABUSE
preventing you from getting or keeping a job • making you ask for money • interfering with work or education • using your credit cards without permission • not working and requiring you to provide support • keeping your name off joint assets

Developed by Roe & Jagodinsky
Adapted from the Power & Control and Equity Wheels developed by the
Domestic Abuse Intervention Project • 206 West Fourth Street • Duluth, Minnesota 55806 • 218/722-4134

DOMESTIC VIOLENCE RESOURCES

Directions: Keep handy the following resources for review. Please note that this information does not include all of the resources available.

National Domestic Violence Hotline

1-800-799-SAFE (7233)

Rape, Abuse & Incest National Network

1-800-656-HOPE

Family Violence Prevention Fund

415-252-8900

National Coalition Against Domestic Violence

303 839 1852

Crime Victims HOTLINE

1-800-621-4673

Rape and Sexual Assault & Incest HOTLINE

212-227-3000

National Resource Center on Domestic Violence

1-800-537-2238

National Resource Center on Domestic Violence

1-800-537-2238

National Clearinghouse on Marital and Date Rape

510-524-1582

National Network to End Domestic Violence

1-800-799-SAFE (7233)

Womenspace National Network to End Violence Against Immigrant Women

609-394-9000

DOMESTIC VIOLENCE POEM

But to Blame

The sky how blue so bright and dark.

These tears I cry for you my sight.

My heart so weak but yet so strong, I can't see myself being alone.

I don't want to think about tomorrow, with all the mistakes with us will follow.

I blame myself for all my sorrow, happiness is what you bring, sorrow had no place in this dream.

I blame myself but it's not true

I fell in love... in love with you.

By: Evelyn Linton

View more poems by Evelyn Linton by going to www.sunshine.weebly.com

CHAPTER 24
ADDICTIONS

ADDICTION

"When you engage in addictive behaviors you are no longer the person who your partner(s) married, you are now the drug."

Olivia L Baylor, LCPC, NCC, DCC

It can be valuable to look into your family upbringing to find out why you began using drugs. If you have suspicions about whether your partner(s) is using drugs, you probably already know the answer to that question. If so, does your partner(s) see the drug use as a problem? If not, then you're beginning the steps to accepting it as a form of your relationship reality. As stated in addictions, 'the first step is admitting that there is a problem'. But what if it's not causing a problem in your life or in your relationship? Relationships can deal with different forms of addictions such as addiction to prescription pills, alcohol, drugs, shopping, unconventional addictions, etc. So how do you handle the addiction? Do you turn your partner away? Do you try to get them help? Do you ignore it and become your own enabler in the relationship? Essentially it won't matter in any of those cases if your partner doesn't:

1. See that they have a problem.

2. Feel as though they need to begin to fix the problem.

When this happens, you can then begin to take the steps to work on the issues in your relationship. Take a look at your family history of addiction, how you cope when you deal with a traumatic or high-risk situation, and how you communicate or ask for help. This is only a brief overview of addiction, if you feel as though you have an addiction contact a local therapist or clinic that specializes in addiction.

STEPS TO TAKE WITH ADDICTION

Directions: Review the following methods to make the necessary changes to addiction.

Admit that you have a problem

Ask for help from family and friends

Remove yourself from addiction (friends/family/ relationships)

SEEK HELP!

What are some other steps that you can take?

_____

_____

_____

_____

ADDICTION WORKSHEET

Directions: Read the vow closely and complete. Complete this worksheet separately, then take time this evening or this week to discuss your answers.

Dear (Insert your name here),

I vow to come to you when I feel like I want to engage in addictive behaviors. When I do come to you, I vow to listen, respect and get help. This I promise to you as my partner(s) in this relationship.

I acknowledge that the following in true. I have a history with using drugs, alcohol or other addictive vices. My addiction is:

_____.

In my family, I have a family history of addiction, or addictive behaviors. Their addiction is/was

_____.

I know that I need to change this and make myself stronger for the sake of our relationship(s).

Signed

_____

WARNING SIGNS ADDICTION WORKSHEET

Directions: Read the warning signs closely. Complete this worksheet separately, then take time this evening or this week to discuss your answers.

1. *Withdrawal symptoms*
   You may notice a physiological change in your partner(s). Some changes include sweating, shaking, rocking, scratching of their arm or body excessively etc.

2. *Change in finances*
   If you notice that your partner(s) is having issues with maintaining funds or are not able to explain why funds are missing.

3. *Addictive peers*
   If you notice a change in your partner(s) friends. They may begin to interact with peers who use substances.

4. *Isolation*
   Your partner(s) may begin to withdrawal to themselves and not interact with others.

5. *Anger/outburst*
   Your partner(s) may lash out to you depending on if they're able to use their substances or not.

6. *Change in appearance*
   Your partner(s) may drastically lose weight, have needle like bruises on their arms, red eyes, loss of hair or teeth.

©Olivia L Baylor LCPC, NCC, DCC

YOU DID IT!

You finished the entire workbook!!!!

How do you feel?

_____

_____

_____

When reviewing your answers with your partner(s) what were some of the things that you learned?

_____

_____

_____

Go back to the beginning of the book and look at your two goals. Did you accomplish it with this workbook?

_____

_____

_____

What were some of the things that you felt were missed in the workbook?

_____

_____

_____

If you want to give me feedback on the book or feel that I missed some items, please let me know. Email me at baylorbook@gmail.com

Thank you and good luck as you begin the journey into your marriage/unity!

Made in the USA
Monee, IL
27 April 2021